D0864594

THE FINGER OF GOD

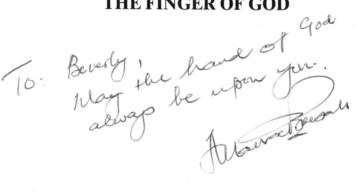

To: Beverly,
May the hand of God
always be upon you.

THE FINGER OF GOD

Sermons on Faith and
Socio-Political Responsibility

Allan Boesak

*Translated from the Afrikaans
by Peter Randall*

ORBIS BOOKS
Maryknoll, New York 10545

Second Printing, December 1982

The Catholic Foreign Mission Society of America (Maryknoll) recruits and trains people for overseas missionary service. Through Orbis Books Maryknoll aims to foster the international dialogue that is essential to mission. The books published, however, reflect the opinions of their authors and are not meant to represent the official position of the society.

Originally published as *Die Vinger Van God,* copyright © 1979 by Allan Boesak, published by Ravan Press, Johannesburg, Republic of South Africa

This translation copyright © 1982 by Orbis Books, Maryknoll, NY 10545

Manufactured in the United States of America

Manuscript Editor: William E. Jerman

Library of Congress Cataloging in Publication Data

Boesak, Allan Aubrey, 1946-
  The finger of God.

  Translation of: Die vinger van God.
  1. Christianity and justice—Sermons. 2. Church and race relations—South Africa—Sermons. 3. Reformed Church—Sermons. 4. Sermons, English—Translations from Afrikaans. 5. Sermons, Afrikaans
BR115.J8B6213   261.8'0968   81-16943
ISBN 0-88344-135-7 (pbk.)   AACR2

To
Theo and Helen Kotze,
whose lives witness to the power
of the word of God

Contents

Foreword

Allan Boesak's *The Finger of God* is an imperative resource for every sincere and serious preacher. These sermons have few equals, and no superiors: in their integrity and intelligence and in their imaginative, evocative, and provocative thrust and content. They confront both preacher and listener with the searching question of the integrity of their own steadfastness in bringing "every thought into captivity to the obedience of Christ" (2 Cor. 10:5). At least every preacher ought to read the Introduction, and at least one sermon, before every preparation for the weekly proclamation of the Gospel.

In marked contrast, most sermons these days are notably irrelevant, and, with few exceptions, books of sermons are dull readings. Sermons—even carefully crafted ones—are nearly always event-less. They are a compound of either the obvious and the trivial, or the learned and the commonplace—or both—on the move from the latitudinous to the platitudinous. Everybody likes to hear what everybody knows—and effectively dismisses as not worth bothering about.

Not so with *The Finger of God*. The sermons exhibit, in a rare and remarkable way, the convicting and transforming reality and power of the Bible in judging, illuminating, and renewing human life. Seldom have I read, or heard, a more eloquent, sobering, and persuasive account of the radical and fulfilling difference that the presence of Jesus of Nazareth *in* the human story makes *to* the human story. Allan Boesak belongs in the company of the great preachers of the Christian church, who have found in Jesus of Nazareth the authentic voice of Moses and the Prophets, and in Paul of Tarsus and John of Patmos formative hearers and doers of that voice. Boesak's is a contemporary voice, joining in a single chorus of affirmation that "the Word of God is that which strikes the conscience!" (Luther)

Responsible Christian preaching does not seek to promote the unintelligible ecstasy of glory. On the contrary, the focus is upon the always contemporary experience of the crucifixion and resurrection of Jesus, upon the "bearing about in the body the death of Jesus, so that the life of Jesus may also be manifested in our bodies" (2 Cor. 4:10). Consequently, the significant themes of Christian proclamation, teaching, faith, and life are all here. In sequence, we are invited and urged to come to terms with trust, authority, faith, doubt and hope; with the renewing power of the Spirit, estrangement, resurrection; with anxiety, reconciliation, the Kingdom of God; and with the peace in the world which the world cannot give, the kingship of Christ, and, in conclusion, with the test case of justice. How should it or could it be otherwise?

Early on in the South African struggle, Alan Paton sent a "Cry, Beloved Country!" flaming across the world. In this compact and gripping volume, Allan Boesak joins his fellow-countryman, and sends a cry across the world from and for a church and country, both deeply beloved! In so doing, a poignant prophecy of James Baldwin—that White America would regain its soul through Black America—begins to find its fulfillment. For these sermons make transparent and inescapable the fact that the black context of South Africa is the human context of the world.

—*Paul Lehmann*

Preface

It is with great hesitation that I have prepared these sermons for publication. Only the repeated requests of many persons—friends, colleagues, and students—persuaded me to take this step.

Some theologians never publish their sermons. Their position is understandable: a sermon is for a particular congregation, in a particular situation, at a particular time. It is delivered within an intimate community in which the word of God and other words are accepted and understood in a particular way. This community and this intimacy are sacrificed in publishing.

Furthermore, in a sermon you give something of yourself away. There is an element of personal danger. You make yourself vulnerable, because you are clothing your person, your convictions, your faith, in the very defenselessness of the gospel itself. Your theologizing is thus taken out of the safe cubicle of theoretical contemplation and concretized for the congregation. And so all the gaps and the flaws are revealed. To the whole congregation.

Above all, a sermon has to do with the concreteness of the gospel of Jesus Christ. It is precisely this concreteness that arouses opposition from sinful humankind whose feeling of certainty and power may be assailed, whose dignity may be damaged because it has to subordinate itself to the word of God. And if public officials are addressed with evangelical directness, it can indeed be dangerous.

Hence, to go ahead and publish sermons (of this nature) perhaps indicates a certain foolishness. This I readily accept. But there is more to it: there is such a thing as being overwhelmed by the gospel, being swept away by the truth of the word and by reality. There is an obligation to proclaim the word for the people—persons of flesh and blood, with anxieties and longings, dreams and desires, joys and sorrows; persons who place their hope in the God who became flesh.

Most of these sermons were prepared for student congregations on the campuses of the University of the Western Cape, the Peninsula Technical College, and the Bellville Training College. These students kept my feet firmly on earth with their critical approach, their reactions and discussions. It is not necessary to prove that the preacher of the word needs such critique. Hence my gratitude.

All the sermons in this collection have the same theme: the socio-political responsibility of the Christian. They have been specially chosen with this in mind. As is argued in the Introduction, the ethical realm is certainly not the only one that is supposed to be gone into in preaching. But it represents the most gaping lacuna in our preaching in South Africa. In addition, the questions that are being asked ever more urgently in the black community cannot any longer be ignored by the preacher.

I do not pretend that this small collection exhausts the full richness of the gospel. Far from it. But I do want to emphasize: this is how one preacher understands the gospel, with reference to South Africa's socio-political reality, and this is how he himself professes the kingship of Jesus Christ in this context.

If it helps others to a renewed faith, or even to an awakening of faith, if it helps some, in the midst of great confusion, to find comfort, direction, and perhaps even inspiration, then this effort will have achieved its goal.

Introduction: Relevant Preaching in a Black Context

The Crisis in the Pulpit

It is now widely acknowledged that a crisis as never before is centering on the pulpit. In South Africa and elsewhere questions about preaching and preachers have proliferated. It is being asked whether the "traditional" form of preaching is still valid or whether we should change to newer, more effective forms of communicating the word of God.

Theologians who pose these questions do not stand alone, nor can they be accused of "liberalistic" views. They pose these questions precisely because of a growing dissatisfaction by church-goers with the sermons they hear.

This probing into the sermon—as regards its form as well as its content—is a good thing. It is about time that preachers were obliged to look at their preaching—and themselves—not only by the academic world but by concerned, critical church members as well.

I do not intend to discuss here all the dimensions of the debate on the form of communicating the word of God, however interesting that might be. I will make it easy for myself by confessing simply that I still find the "traditional" form of preaching—namely, the proclamation of the word by a preacher to a community of believers—the best way to communicate the word.

This does not mean, of course, that the preacher has to have the floor all the time, or that I do not take seriously the necessity of discussion before and after the sermon. I certainly do not claim that the *written* word is not an effective form of communicating the word of God to others. I simply want to say that I am not

1

convinced that the "new" forms of communication—drama, dance, or whatever—can take the place of the "traditional" sermon.[1]

In some other countries the crisis in traditional preaching has to do with empty pews, diminishing memberships, problems with regard to personnel, and the like. Colin Morris also mentions the "drastic shift from church to action-oriented Christianity" and the problems that arose for the church through the new, radical theologies typified by the *Honest to God* and *The Death of God* furors.[2] All this has very much undermined the traditional form of being the church in the world, and therefore the traditional form of preaching.

In the black Christian community of South Africa we also face an undeniable crisis in preaching, even though the reasons for it elsewhere are not necessarily duplicated in our context. There is not such a drop in church attendance, for instance, that we find it necessary to change the essential character of our "traditional" services. No, the present crisis in our preaching centers almost exclusively on the *content* of the sermon.

In my opinion this becomes clear in the inability of most black preachers to speak the word of God forcefully and relevantly to the black Christian community living in an ever changing situation. It is the formidable task of the black preacher to speak the word in such a way that it comforts, inspires, and gives life, for black Christians seek a word that witnesses to the presence of God in their lives. A word that shows a way out of the darkness of oppression, poverty, and misery. A word that is an inspiration to active participation in God's struggle for justice and liberation, yet at the same time is not itself an expression of demagogy. A word that holds on to the truth that God is on the side of the oppressed and that he, if they put their trust in him, will deliver them from the power of the oppressor—as he did in the past. By the same token this word should not be a homiletical lullaby[3] that will gently rock them into believing that "everything'll be all right," and eventually rock them to eternal sleep.

At this point the black preacher realizes what Colin Morris has so correctly observed: "Preaching is not difficult: it is strictly impossible."[4]

It becomes clearer and clearer that the expectations just

described have so cornered the black preacher that we are justified in speaking of a crisis. To be sure, the crisis is not constituted
by any inadequacy on the part of the word of God, but by the
inability and unwillingness of the preacher to preach this word
honestly and fearlessly within the context of the black experience
in South Africa.

Factors Contributing to the Seriousness of the Crisis

It is necessary to look a little more deeply into this situation and
especially at the factors that to my mind are responsible for it.

First of all we must think about the new political situation. The
last six to seven years have seen profound and rapid changes in the
black community in South Africa. These changes are perceptible
not so much in tangible political structures as in a new political
consciousness.

This consciousness reached a peak in 1976 when thousands of
young persons and students took to the streets in ardent protest
against the government's policy of apartheid and everything this
evil system represents. These events ushered in a new phase in
South Africa's political history.

Of those young persons, and later also their parents who became increasingly involved in the protests, there were many who
belonged to Christian churches. Many of them are still in the
church, but now with a heightened and highly sensitized political
consciousness, with probing, critical questions about the nature
and witness of the church and therefore also about the nature and
content of preaching. They are young persons with an experience
of life far beyond their years, an experience born of their active
and personal engagement in the struggle for liberation and their
God-given humanity.

It is my contention that these events caught the Christian
churches in South Africa unawares. The churches do not yet
know how to accommodate the special concerns and drives of this
new, politically conscious generation.

The second factor follows upon the first. This new political
consciousness gives rise to new existential questions in the minds
of churchgoers. Foremost is the question: who am I? What does it
mean—to me as a Christian, to me as a human—that a govern-

ment that I did not have the opportunity to vote for treats me as a "colored," or a "Bantu," or an "Indian," instead of as a human being, a South African citizen? How can a Christian be at peace with humiliation and dehumanization when God has created us with equal dignity? Is there an obligation of obedience to a government that makes unjust laws—laws that are, to quote the Scottish Confession, "repugnant to the Word of God"? Do I have the right to resist, and if so, how? What are Christians to do when they have to live under oppression— *and* when oppression claims to be "Christian"?

When black Christians gather in church to hear the will of God for their lives, it is these and similar questions that besiege their minds. Preaching, if it is to be authentic, will have to focus the searchlight of the gospel on all these questions.

A third factor. The new political consciousness, and the decision for solidarity with the oppressed that we call black consciousness, have brought a new sense of responsibility into the black community. This, plus their active involvement in struggle, have dissipated almost completely their traditional diffidence vis-à-vis the church and its official representatives. Office-holders are no longer judged by their office and the authority vested in it; the office and the authority it claims are now measured in terms of the active participation of officeholders in the struggle for liberation.

Talk of the supposed chasm between the church and the world, between the gospel and politics, is no longer credible: young persons are beginning to suspect that the relationship might be closer than can be admitted by the ecclesiastical leadership. They realize more and more that, although the church and politics are not identical, they seem to have the same agenda. The young want the church to put points on the agenda that are in accord with the demands of the gospel of Jesus Christ even if this may mean that "politics" would be embarrassed. It is for this reason that there is debate in the church about its role in society, about its prophetic witness (or lack of it), and about the identification of the church with those who suffer in the community it proposes to serve.

All of this brings out the fourth factor—namely, the inadequacy of pietistic traditions and preaching in the church. It is becoming clear—painfully clear—that the pietistic, other-worldly theology preached in most black churches (whether by a "missionary" or a black minister) cannot provide the answers the new situation demands. Moreover, it is becoming clear that this kind of theology is often the handmaid of authoritarian structures that preserve the status quo within the church, with the result that the church is being held back to an era that has irrevocably passed. This puts the church in the unenviable position that its leadership—ministers, councils, synods, executive bodies—is being estranged from the church, that is, the people. This is a situation that must soon become untenable.

It must also be pointed out that the church in South Africa has not been able to deal adequately with new situations caused by black consciousness within the churches. Too many churches are still completely controlled by whites, who often are defenders of the status quo, who resist meaningful change in the church with all their white might, which in our situation can be considerable.

This state of affairs also makes it impossible for the church to react creatively to the discovery by black Christians that their humanity, contrary to what they have been taught by our South African way of life, is constituted by their blackness and that this liberating discovery has far-reaching consequences for their whole lives.

It is true: most whites who serve black churches find it nearly impossible to work with awakened, liberated, independent-thinking black persons. Although these blacks do not deny white Christians a role in the black church, they do deny them the role of the ones who, by virtue of their color, should always have the last word. The confrontation that results from all this is both necessary and unavoidable, and it will continue until whites have learned to love blacks—including those who are not helpless.

The final factor that we want to discuss here is found in the understandable fear of black preachers to proclaim the word of God clearly and honestly to their people. In the life of the black preacher this fear is a bitter, shameful reality. The white government of South Africa has a vast array of oppressive laws that have an intimidating effect on the preacher. A sermon that is too clear may land the preacher in the hands of the dreaded Security Police, because such a sermon could, within the definition of the law, be anything from "instigation" to "terrorism."[5]

To preach the word of God relevantly in South Africa is to walk through a minefield—blindfolded.

This has the unhappy result that even when preachers (assuming that they are able to exchange their other-worldly theology for biblical theology) arrive at the point of preaching the truth about the socio-political situation their people live in, they face the possibility of diverse forms of prosecution. All of this is a very formidable barrier to a form of preaching that would take the black condition seriously, and to the promises of God to the oppressed who trust in him.

Thus the vital question, "What does God have to say about my life, my whole life?" is in danger of not being posed at all in the black congregation. The only thing left for the searching Christian who still comes to church is amazement, disappointment, and, in the end, frustration—to the extent even that young black persons today begin to leave the church, for they see it as "irrelevant."[6] But through it all, the command of Jesus to his church still stands: "You shall be my witnesses!" (Acts 1:8).

The Unavoidable Task

Any church that disregards this command of Jesus will surely pay the price. The church has no option about interpreting what the Spirit says. Preaching is not only the unavoidable task of the church, it is the task of the church *par excellence.*

Preaching is the proclamation of the word of God, the gospel, to the people. This is our first, partial definition. Through preaching the witness of those who have seen and believed is recounted again and again to those "who have not yet seen and believed." Although this is done in human words, preaching is not a merely human enterprise. Through divine intervention (not human ingenuity!) preaching becomes a revelatory event.

This truth should fill preachers with dread and more than a little hesitancy. Who are they to bring the word of God to others? Whichever way we look at it, preachers' words are simply inadequate to give life to the full import of the gospel. The preacher is, as Paul so aptly put it, no more than an earthen vessel.

But there is another side to this. The preacher proclaims the word of God, a word endowed with an authority that cannot be neutralized or denied, not even by the stumbling words of the preacher. Preachers derive their authority not from the people, nor even from the church. They derive it from the One whose word they may proclaim. I cannot escape the miracle here: God speaks to his people through the words of a mere human being.

It is in this connection that Barth spoke of the "mystery of preaching." Herein lies the truth that the sermon is neither the prattle of pious-sounding words, nor a well-structured oration. The sermon is an event, and again not because of the preacher, but because of the truth that is authenticated in the proclamation of the word. God wants to use a mere human being, not an angel, to proclaim his word, and this causes acute embarrassment in the preacher.

All preachers know that most of the time they find themselves caught up in their own situation, with a particular background and a particular understanding of the gospel and of the reality of their own life. How does one keep the two apart: instrument of God and a particular person living in a particular situation?

We shall have to be honest and admit that preachers cannot be divorced from their life experiences, from the situations in which they live. In the preparation of their sermons and in the formulation of their theology there is a host of factors that influence them. What is true for theology is true for preaching: it is situational. It is the unenviable task of preachers to wrestle honestly with the word of God to experience its critical power, for themselves and for the people they preach to—but always within the situation and the experience of their people, so that the preaching will be understandable and relevant.

The Relevant Word

How to speak the word of God so that it is relevant to one's hearers may seem a simple matter, but it involves a complex of problems the preacher cannot afford to ignore. Preaching is the proclamation of the gospel in a language that can be understood by persons in a specific situation. This is our final, full definition.

H. M. Kuitert speaks of intelligibility and relevance in the same breath, and correctly so: "To speak a comprehensible language [from the pulpit] is to speak in such a way that listeners experience what they hear as of vital importance for their concrete existence in the world."[7] If the sermon is not directed to the real, everyday lives of its hearers, they really do not "hear" it or "understand" it; it is not relevant, for it ignores their deepest needs.

It is exactly here that the shoe pinches. What is "relevant preaching" for black Christians? It is preaching that addresses their deepest existential problems, preaching that speaks to the whole of their existence. For blacks, this means that the preacher must address not merely their being in the world, but their being *black* in the world.[8]

Relevant preaching cannot be the kind of preaching that has become the tradition in South Africa: a pietistic, pie-in-the-sky-when-you-die theology that passes for "gospel truth." That kind of preaching turns Christians into "displaced persons" because it continually transports them into the hereafter and has absolutely no answers for the here and now. Relevant preaching certainly has nothing at all to do with the kind of preaching that specializes in "getting at" its hearers with a spiritual whip to satisfy what T. H. Reik has correctly called "Christian masochism,"[9] that dark longing within the hearts of so many Christians to be flogged into the arms of Jesus—or into the fires of hell.

The sober truth is, for black Christians in South Africa today, relevant preaching is ethical preaching; more precisely, political preaching. Let us take a closer look at this. White preachers in their white churches can afford to speak placidly about "eternal truths" that are not bound to any particular place and any particular time. They can, even today, work themselves into a lather about miniskirts, and whether women should be allowed to wear hats in church. They can afford not to be too specific when they speak about social justice. After all, it is an easy thing to preach for oneself.

It is a different story for black preachers. Their congregations are part of the community of the oppressed. Their white colleagues reach to persons who have political and economic power; the government is their government. It is their parishioners who make the laws, and white preachers also enjoy the benefits of those laws.

Black preachers preach to persons who do not have the vote. Among their parishioners there are many who live without their spouses, or without their children, not because they want to, but because of the law of the land. Their parishioners live in those places euphemistically called "housing schemes." Places where they have been forced to go by law, where none of them has yet succeeded in feeling at home. Places with a sorry reputation throughout the world—Soweto, Bonteheuwel, Langa, Dimbasa. To say nothing of the squatter camps.

Their hearers are the ones who have to say *baas* to a white man in order to ensure bread for their children. And then they have to deal with the humiliation and afterward the tension and embarrassment—who really likes to have to say "massa" to someone else?[10]

Black preachers know that fellowship, reconciliation, and love are themes that involve special problems for them. This is so not only because they fear God, but also because their congregations have exchanged an innocent faith for a critical faith. To thank God for "our Christian government" does not come so easily to the lips of black preachers as to those of white preachers. Black preachers know that black Christians question the Christian motives and convictions of the present government. Their prayer, when they think of the government, is rather a prayer for deliverance.

To be sure, there are some white preachers who realize that social justice is an evangelical demand and that they *have* to preach about it. Often, however, these sermons are so circumspect that they contain neither a reprimand for the government, nor comfort for those who suffer. Again, black preachers cannot afford this. They cannot be blind to the suffering of their people. Their preaching is permeated with a sense of urgency because they know that there is very little time left.

Apart from the fact that they personally experience the pain and humiliation caused by discrimination, and apart from the fact that they have firsthand knowledge of the formidable white power structures, they also know only too well that the oppressor always has more time than they have. Because of all this, black preaching discovers dimensions in the gospel that the white preacher can come to know only through genuine conversion.

This difference in observation, in interpretation of the gospel and of the reality in which we live, is the result of the political situation in our country, a structuring in which the Christian church is also held prisoner. It is a sinful structure that has contaminated the church of Christ in South Africa. It should not only be unmasked as sinful but fought against with all our might. This is why we say: relevant preaching is political preaching.

Relevant Preaching is Ethical (Political) Preaching

There is no reason to be afraid of this. In South Africa our lives are completely dominated by government politics and it causes social and spiritual deprivation on a massive scale. The white government's policy of apartheid not only poisons social life in South Africa, it also causes bitterness and alienation, distrust and suspicion, among individuals. It obstructs the realization of reconciliation. It controls human lives with a frightening totality.[11] It has no respect for the sanctity of marriage and family life. It makes a blasphemous claim of being Christian. Worst of all: it plays God in the lives of human beings.

Sunday after Sunday the churches in the black community are filled with worshipers who no longer deny that they are being oppressed. Their growing political and human consciousness makes it impossible for them to shirk their responsibility with a bland, religious innocence.

On top of it all there is the confusion in the minds of these Christians caused by the fact that a so-called Christian government is responsible for their dire situation. The confusion is heightened by the sad and painful truth that there are churches and individual Christians who defend this system as the will of God for South Africa, using arguments from the same gospel that for blacks has become God's incomparable word of liberation.

In such a situation, preaching that does not include God's will for the socio-political reality in which a people lives is not only unintelligible and irrelevant, it is also dishonest and delinquent. It is then that proclamation of the word becomes nothing more than the repetition of sanctimonious trivialities and what should be service to God becomes self-serving idolatry.

The term "political preaching" is a risky one. To many it conjures up visions of an attack on the "pure gospel" by "modern, liberalistic" theological forces. In spite of the risks involved, the times demand that we be honest. That is the reason why we use this term. With "political preaching" we highlight that much neglected sphere of ethical preaching that is still struggling for its rightful place in preaching.

We do not mean that preachers are to give a lecture on politics, or (even worse) that they preach politics. They preach the word of God and the demands of the gospel with regard to social and political questions. They bring socio-political reality under the critique of the word of God. Political preaching is a necessary aspect of preaching. It does not exhaust the riches of the word of God, but without it there can be no "full gospel" either.

Consider what E.L. Smelik says about ethical preaching:

> Preaching without ethical consequences eventually loses its right to exist. It loses touch with those who live in the world. For whoever lives in the world has to make ethical decisions. Whoever eliminates the ethical dimension of preaching gives up the obedience to the word. Those who do this betray their divine calling.[12]

We fear that there is more than just a little hypocrisy in the resistance to ethical (political) preaching. Christians and churches have always been involved in politics. The silence that some want the church to maintain on these issues means that they are affirming the status quo. But there is more that we must say about this.

Preaching is the proclamation, so we have said, of the gospel to persons living in a particular situation. It is a proclamation that covers all of life. The preacher does not preach anything but Christ. The question immediately arises: who and what is Jesus Christ for us today? How are we to confess him today?[13]

Preaching is the proclamation of the kingly rule of Christ over all of life. It is the proclamation of the salvation of God that has become real in Jesus the Messiah. Preaching is the announcement of God's judgment on sin, both personal sin and the sin deeply embedded in social, economic, and political structures.

Preaching is also the announcement of God's promises of grace and forgiveness for those who repent. It is a call to *metanoia,* conversion, to a restructuring of our lives and the societies we live in. It is the proclamation of the word of him who is Liberator, whose will it is to make human life human, and to keep it human in the world.[14]

Preaching is the proclamation of the word of the God who is one and indivisible. The confession of the lordship of Christ over all of life must be heard again in our preaching, as a protest against the departmentalization of life, and as a plea for faith in the God of the Bible who cannot be divided, and whose power can be neither deferred nor denied.

To "keep politics out of religion" (or out of preaching) is to break up the wholeness of life. It is to put an impermissible limitation on the restorative and renovative work of the Holy Spirit.

Compartmentalization, so writes Max Warren, is the essence of heathenism:

> Without realizing it we have drifted back into the old polytheism against which the prophets of the Lord waged their great warfare. The real essence of paganism is that it divides the various concerns of human life into compartments. There is one god for the soil; there is another god of the desert. The god of wisdom is quite different from the god of wine. If a man wants to marry he must pray at one temple; if he wants to make war he must take his sacrifice elsewhere. All this is precisely where the modern paganism of our secular society has brought us today. Certain portions of our life we call religious. Then we are Christians. We use a special language. . . . We call that our Christianity—and there we stop. We turn to another department of life we call politics. Now we think in quite different terms. Our liturgy is the catchwords of the daily press. Our divine revelation is the nine o'clock news. Our creed is "I believe in democracy." Our incentive is the fear of— we're not sure what. But it certainly isn't the fear of the Lord.[15]

Warren is right. For this is the way too many Christians live. God is for our religious life. But then there is another god for politics, another for the economy, and still another for the sphere of private life. These persons (who still call themselves Christians and who still go to church) want the preacher to respect this pagan way of life, and woe unto the preacher who dares to break down these sacralized walls!

The result is predictable. The well-known argument "business is business and politics is politics" acquires the authority of a biblical axiom. In the end God is tolerated in his area: that of religion. The other areas become completely autonomous, with their own laws, their own way of doing things, completely shut off to the Torah and the prophets.

But there is another result of this stance we have to deal with. It is the fruitless polarization between the personal and the social, between personal needs and socio-economic needs. Preachers may concern themselves with the first; their concern with the second is not tolerated. As if the man who has lost his wife is entitled to God's mercy and help, but the peson who is exploited by unjust structures could be denied that privilege! To preach about the loneliness of persons in our secular world is all right; to preach about the terrible estrangement that is the result of apartheid is wrong, because it is "politics." As if the one is less real than the other! As if "politics" would have the right to withdraw itself from the judgment (and the mercy!) of the Lord to whom is given all power in heaven and on earth (Matt. 28:18)!

A. A. van Ruler has extremely valuable insights on this point. He rejects unequivocally a complete separation of politics and Christian faith. He calls parliament, where the laws are made and vital political decisions are taken, the "beauty salon where makeup is put on the face of life."[16] But van Ruler immediately goes on to say:

> But let us not discard the face as unimportant. . . . The face is part of the human body. The exterior of the political organization of the community is an integral part of human existence! It is in these "exterior realities" that persons express themselves . . . and communality [being part of a community] is just as essential, just as constitutive as individuality. And in realizing this, community justice is just as essential as love. Politics is concerned with laws, and for this very reason politics is a sacred business.[17]

Besides, Reformed Christians ought to know better. They
know that Calvin had argued conclusively that it is not possible to
separate politics and "spiritual truth." At least, this is what he
writes to the king, and he continues his argument:

> Your first task as a ruler is to build your kingdom on justice.
> But if you are not interested in religion, if you allow yourself
> to be misled . . . you make of yourself a participant in injus-
> tice and your government will be nothing else but gang-
> sterism.[18]

These are hard words. According to André Biler in his unique
study on the social and political insights of Calvin, there were
those who considered Calvin a troublemaker, a "disturber of the
public order." This is an accusation that those who, by their Christian witness, today attack apartheid have to face time and time
again.

Calvin's answer was that he believed that Christians should always be a disturbance to the social order to a certain extent, because "explicitly they unmask the injustices of the society in
which they live, for they take the word of God seriously and act
upon its demands."[19]

"The real troublemakers," Calvin writes—and his words seem
as if directed to the South African government in 1980—"are
those who prolong religious and social disorder by protecting it!
Those reactionary conservatives who through their injustice and
violence hold onto the lie, and who refuse to listen to the truth."[20]

Reformed Christians know that political institutions do not exist autonomously. They are not a law unto themselves, not having
to take the law of God into account. Scripture is the norm for all
ethics, for all human actions. Political traditions, economic and
social structures are not divinely ordained, unchangeable and
eternal. They all fall under the critique of the word of God. And
the church, through its preaching and other forms of prophetic
witness, must formulate this critique and probe the realities of our
lives for the truth of the gospel message.

But we also have an example in the biblical proclamation itself.
The prophets of old never hesitated to speak God's word for the

whole of life. They were unflinching and uncompromising in their confrontation with kings and rulers with regard to social justice issues. Moreover, the words and actions of Jesus the Messiah even today have profound political ramifications. The astounding concreteness of his demands does not leave us much room for the privatization of Christian faith.

The preacher who wishes to be true to the word of God has no alternative but to speak just as clearly and just as relevantly. The proclamation of the word loses its meaning when it comes to heavens outside their historical reality. And politics is just as much a part of their historical reality as is family life. Political preaching is not only desirable, it is also necessary and, in our situation, imperative.

Preaching and Authenticity

We must now turn to yet another aspect of our subject: preaching, if it is to be heeded, must not only be solid proclamation of the word, it should not only be preceded by thorough study and honest exegesis, it must also be authentic. For this reason preaching cannot be merely a repetition of dogmatic truths, or the senseless chatter of pious generalities. Authenticity lies in the correct combination of exposition of the word, sensitivity to the situation of the congregation, and the inner conviction resulting from a personal experience of God's liberation in the life of the preacher.

The authentic preacher understands this and therefore is willing to preach the word fearlessly and, if need be, to suffer for the sake of the Lord. Martin Luther King, Jr., understood this and expressed it in words grown out to cosmic proportions:

> Even they try to kill you, you develop the inner conviction that there are some things so dear, some things so precious, some things so eternally true that they are worth dying for. And if a man has not found something that he will die for, he isn't fit to live![21]

Of course, not every black preacher can be a Martin Luther King, and not everyone is called to such a dramatic ministry, but some of this is true for our situation and the reality of suffering for the sake of the Lord is already being experienced by many Christians in this country.

To be authentic is to be true to the experience of the persons who listen to the sermon. Does this mean, then, that their experience becomes the sermon? Or put in another way: if apartheid controls so totally the lives of a congregation, does one preach about apartheid? The answer is an unequivocal *no,* but preachers cannot ignore the reality of apartheid and what it means for those who listen to them. Apartheid is not the word of God and it cannot eliminate or manipulate that word. It does, however, form the framework in which hearers live, and as such the sermon has to take cognizance of the situation caused by apartheid.

Authenticity has another aspect. Preachers can talk about liberation only if they themselves are liberated persons. They can preach God's liberation to others only if they themselves know and understand what it means to be liberated from hatred, fear, prejudice, and the compulsion to survive at all costs. They can speak of solidarity with the oppressed only if they themselves are not afraid to identify themselves with the struggle of those who in many respects have less than they do. They can speak of the hope of the suffering only when they themselves are willing to be honest with their people in their role as children of God who seek the kingdom of God and its truth for the socio-political realities of our world.

Authentic preachers know that they belong to the church. Their preaching stands within a tradition, within a historical community, confessing its faith in the living One who is its Lord. That is why the "we" of the preacher is neither editorial nor royal; it is confessional.[22]

Preachers do not stand aloof from the church. Even their criticism of the church because of its failure to be true to its Christ in the area of social concern does not separate them from the church. Their criticism should not be the result of malicious pleasure, but rather the result of their love and concern for the church. They serve the church with a loving and critical solidarity.

In the final analysis, preachers are servants of the word of God. Their authority, as we have argued before, is not given them by the church, but by the Lord of the church. To accord dogmas and traditions the same authority as the word of God is sin and dangerously arrogant. Preachers know that the word of God has the last say, and that this holds true for them as well as for the church. They do not only accept the authority of the word, they live by it.

A Last Word

Let us reiterate that everything we have said thus far does not mean that the sermon will be pure politics. I am not saying that preaching should be ethical Sunday after Sunday. I do argue, however, for preaching that speaks to the *whole* person and to *all* of life. The demands and the promises of the gospel are valid for the whole and the wholeness of our existence, and the full consequences of the gospel should be made clear to Christians.

Preachers will not try to work out detailed political formulas and ram them down the throats of their listeners. But they must measure political programs and social realities by the demands for justice and liberation in the gospel. They proclaim a word that is continually at loggerheads with the reality of the world and always at a critical distance from human planning. They will have to remind their churches that the kingdom of God is not to be equated with a just social order.

Preaching is proclamation of the demands of the kingdom that in Jesus Christ has come and yet is still to come in all its fulness. The church must proclaim through its preaching the ethical demands of the kingdom that in Jesus Christ has come and yet is still to come in all its fulness. The church must proclaim through its preaching that the ethical demands of the kingdom of God are not merely words but also deeds, not only sound but also reality (H.N. Ridderbos). Preachers who are not true to this truth betray their calling.

But Micaiah answered: "As Yahweh lives, what Yahweh says to me, that I will utter!" (1 Kings 22:14).

1

Whence Comes Our Help?

Sacred Trust
Apropos of October 19, 1977 [1]

> *In the thirty-ninth year of his reign Asa was diseased in his*
> *feet, and his disease became severe; yet even in his disease he*
> *did not seek the Lord, but sought help from the physicians*
> *[2 Chronicles 16:12].*

Things were going badly for Israel. We are speaking here of
Israel in its diminished form: after Solomon's death the one people of God was divided into two segments—Israel in the north (the
kingdom of the ten tribes) and Judah in the south (the kingdom of
the two tribes). Hostility had reached the point where the two
brothers—Asa, king of Judah, and Baasha, king of Israel—rose
up against each other and tried to destroy each other in a senseless
war.

In addition, an entirely new development occurred between the
two of them: an outsider, a heathen foreigner—Ben-hadad, king
of Aram (an ancient name for Syria)—was called in to support
one brother against the other.

Reflecting on this, the psalmist chokes; his joy turns to bitterness. His canticle on brotherhood turns to sarcasm: "Behold, how good and pleasant it is when brothers dwell in unity!" (Ps. 133:1). The oil on Aaron's beard drips as heavy as blood in the dust of the holy city.

Baasha, greatly strengthened by his alliance with Ben-hadad, king of Syria, rose up against Asa. Asa recognized the danger and wanted to obviate it.

But how?

He hit upon the idea of bribing the king of Syria and thus persuade him to help him, Asa, instead of his brother. And Asa bought over Ben-hadad with gold and silver that he took from the temple.

Unlike the author of 1 Kings 15, where this history is also recorded, the chronicler—the author of the Books of Chronicles— does not speak of "the treasures that were left over." The chronicler relentlessly exposes the king's machinations. For him it was a case of theft, because the treasures of the temple were not the property of the king; they belonged to God! And with this treasure Asa wanted to bribe Syria to enter into an alliance with him, breaking his alliance with Baasha. And Asa succeeded.

The victory that followed (because with Ben-hadad's help Asa overcame Israel) later put a bitter taste in his mouth. This was because (and how could it be otherwise?) a prophet came to Asa, not to congratulate him on his victory, but to tell him precisely what he had done wrong.

The prophet Hanani took the spark out of Asa's flush of victory by saying to him, in effect: "What you did, Asa, was indeed clever, but it was not wise. It was wrong! You formed an alliance with Ben-hadad, a heathen king. Things will not go well with you, Asa, because you relied on a heathen in place of the Lord your God."

Why does the prophet not have a good word for Asa's obvious political skill? Why does he ignore the reality of politics? Why can he not see that, taking everything into account, it was not such a bad plan, given the fact that Asa sought victory?

The reason is this: the sealing of a pact is a sacred avowal of trust. And for the people of God there already was a pact that stood fast—the pact, the covenant, with Yahweh! Asa, however, overlooked this. In his anxiety he sought the king of Syria. He did not even think of Yahweh, but put his trust in a man who shortly before was prepared to destroy him by fighting on the side of Baasha. Only the size of Asa's money order saved him.

Great princes may bear imposing names; they may show off with strong armies and have far-flung kingdoms; but one must *not* collaborate with them, even if Israel had concluded a pact with them. Only Yahweh is worthy of his people's trust. He had shown himself to be trustworthy throughout the course of history. If Asa had called upon him, he would have shown who had the power in the last instance.

And it was not as if Asa did not know all this. The prophet (2 Chron. 16:7–8) refers to Asa's experience when he had fought shortly before against the Ethiopians. *Then* Asa well knew "whence came his help." *Then* he well knew to place his trust in Yahweh:

> And Asa cried to the Lord his God, "O Lord, there is none like you to help the powerless against the strong. Help us, O Lord our God, for we rely on you and in your name we have come against this multitude. O Lord, you are God; let no man prevail against you" [2 Chron. 14:10].

And we read what happened next: "So the Lord defeated the Ethiopians before Asa and before Judah, and the Ethiopians fled" (2 Chron. 14:11).

But now Asa does not put his trust in Yahweh. Or is his belief perhaps pointed in only one direction? The previous time the threat was from the south; now it is from the north. But does not Asa know, asks the prophet, that the eyes of the Lord scan the whole earth, "to show his might in support of those whose heart is blameless toward him" (2 Chron. 16:9)?

By covenanting with Syria, breaking the covenant with Yahweh, and not trusting God in his politics, Asa, so we read, behaved "foolishly." In the Bible the fool is the one who does not reckon with God, who acts as if God did not exist. He takes account only of earthly powers. He stares blindly at what he sees, and he chooses the weapons with which he thinks he can overcome earthly power and avert danger.

Because he forgets God, he trusts in his own weapons, his own ability, his own allies. And both the chronicler and the prophet proclaim God's judgment on this.

Asa exacerbates the matter: he becomes angry with the prophet and throws him into prison. And those who agree with the prophet and criticize the king's actions he is furious with, and suppresses them too. Once again we see how the established powers react to embarrassing criticism.

But things become even worse. It is as if the chronicler says, "if only that were all!" It was disastrous enough not to trust Yahweh in politics, but even in his illness Asa did not consult Yahweh; he sought help from physicians.

We must not misunderstand this: it is not doctors and medicines that are being preached against. The angry words apply not to the doctors, but to the king. The chronicler is not resorting to a reprisal theory, in the sense that Asa became ill *because* he did not trust God. It is simply mentioned as a matter of fact that Asa, in the thirty-ninth year of his reign, was "diseased in his feet." No, Asa was much more blameworthy because in his illness he apparently relied only on the doctors. In other words, *even then* he still did not know "whence came his help"—namely, from him "who heals all your diseases" (Ps. 103:3).

In the Old Testament sickness was also frequently seen as a "visitation," alloting a time for reflection and contemplation, a time to seek God. This was thus a personal matter that Asa had to put right between himself and God. By the same token, Asa's sickness was also a symbol of the condition in which he and his people found themselves. In the Old Testament illness sometimes symbolizes apostasy, estrangement from Yahweh and one's neighbors, the morass of godlessness into which the people sometimes sank.

So it was with Asa, in his diseased politics *and* his diseased body, without God. And even in this condition, in his fatal illness, he "did not seek the Lord. . . ."

Asa is not dead. He lives on, in our midst. The sins of Asa are not foreign to us. Christians behave today exactly as did Asa. They behave "foolishly." We place our trust in our own efficacy, in our own capabilities. We believe that our organizational skill, our money, and our intellectual prowess are alone sufficient.

Our Trust

Therefore let us not judge Asa too quickly. After all, on what, and in whom, do we place our trust? With whom do we covenant? Even in our churches God is not trusted unconditionally. I am afraid that we begin to think of Yahweh only *after* we have planned, only *after* we have first looked at what we have or do not have, and only *after* considering the possibilities that *we* can see or calculate.

And where do we place our trust in political affairs? Do we trust Yahweh and do we choose the cause of justice for all who share this country with us and who should be treated justly? Or do we silently choose a policy of white/nonwhite integration in the hope that things will improve for *us*—because then, so we argue, we will be treated as *whites?* So it was that someone shared his conviction with me that "the nonwhites" have no other choice than to put their trust—his words!—in the whites because that was where, according to him, "our future" lies.

This seems to me the pinnacle of foolishness: on what do *they* rely—the persons on whom we are supposed to rely? In what does white, Christian South Africa place its trust? Look, they say, the country is being threatened! Disaster is at the threshold! Enemies are all around us! Anxiety fastens its clammy hands around millions of hearts. But what happens then? Instead of seeking out the cause of the threat and eradicating it, instead of ensuring justice and righteousness so that we may have peace, the threat is met with murder and slaughter. The defense budget climbs to an astonishing two billion rand [approx. $2.5 billion]. The only language used is one of threat, or war, and in *Die Burger* the first ominous letter appears: South Africa must make sure, with an atom bomb if necessary, that even America will be afraid to "attack" it.

Consolation for the anxiety gripping many hearts: that must be the reason for the otherwise incomprehensible decision to ban eighteen organizations and to restrict persons, among them ministers of the gospel—thereby destroying all faith in the sincerity of this government.

The answer to the deterioration of human relationships
the black people's rejection of the humiliation and oppress
apartheid is the purchase of yet more guns and an exhortat... to
the *volk* to hold itself in a state of "readiness."

South Africa, too, is summoned to believe the promises of the
word of God and to trust in *them,* just as Israel was summoned by
Isaiah:

> Is not this the fast that I choose:
>   to loose the bonds of wickedness.
>   to undo the thongs of the yoke;
> To let the oppressed go free,
>   and to break every yoke?
> Is it not to share your bread with the hungry
>   and bring the homeless poor into your house;
> When you see the naked, to cover them
>   and not turn your back on your own?
> Then shall your light break forth like the dawn,
>   and your wound shall speedily be healed;
> Your righteousness shall go before you,
>   the glory of the Lord shall be your rear guard.
> Then shall you call and the Lord will answer;
>   you shall cry for help, and he will say:
> Here I am! [Isa. 58:6-9].

Instead of this, white South Africans are advised to place their
trust in yet more "security" laws, in yet more detentions without
trial, in an abominable alliance with injustice and a violence that
can only escalate.

What is the other side of this coin? Is it that we black Christians
increasingly place our trust not in Yahweh the liberator, the God
of the exodus who is also our God, but in the fostering of hatred,
in the hope offered by improved weaponry, in the violence of ret-
ribution, and in a sorry alliance with the enemies of the cross?
Because we have no other choice? Perhaps. But is the tragedy, and
is God's judgment, thereby averted?

How sick our country is! What we see on the outside—
apartheid, humiliation, hatred, suspicion, the destruction of

families, migrant labor—are merely the stinking boils on the surface, symptoms of all that is devouring us internally. Oppression, anxiety, suspicion, and distrust all wreck our chances for authentic reconciliation. And in the meanwhile we remain mute before the misery and we argue in the press about whether women should wear hats in church!

"Even in his disease Asa did not seek the Lord . . ."

May God forgive us! And he will:

Wash yourselves; make yourselves clean; seek justice, correct oppression; defend the fatherless; plead for the widow. Come now, let us reason together, says the Lord: though your sins are like scarlet, they shall be as white as snow; though they are red like crimson, they shall become like wool [Isa. 1:16–18].

It seems to me worth the effort to have faith in *this* God. So do not place your trust in "clever" political schemes that tomorrow or the day after will be revealed as "foolish" in the light of God's judgment. Do not place your trust in what you can amass and the status that you can earn for yourself. Do not place it in human notions that seem attractive today but will crumble away under your feet tomorrow.

Rather place your faith in him whose fidelity and mercy perdure, and whose love is unchanging in Jesus. He can forgive. He can save. He cannot deny himself. And he will be merciful to us.

2

Jesus and Pilate

Authority and Authorities

> *At this Pilate said to him, "So, then, you are a king?" Jesus replied: "It is you who say I am a king. The reason I was born, the reason why I came into the world, is to testify to the truth. Anyone committed to the truth hears my voice."*
> *. . . [Pilate] said to the Jews, "Look at your king!" At this they shouted, "Away with him! Crucify him!" "What!" Pilate exclaimed. "Shall I crucify your king?" The chief priests replied, "We have no king but Caesar" [John 18:37, 19:14–15].*

Anyone reading these verses superficially could be misled into thinking merely what a skillful writer John is. Is it not impressive what he could do with words! The use of language, the skill with which the tension is relentlessly maintained, might persuade one that, as far as John is concerned, there is little more at issue here than simply a play on words.

But clearly much more is involved: readers are mistaken if they do not realize it. What is happening here is crucial in the strictest sense of the word. For John it is infinitely more than a matter of portraying a Jesus to be pitied. Great decisions are involved in this episode in the passion narrative.

It is clear that Jesus has been summoned here before the seat of Pontius Pilate to be judged by the representative of the Roman emperor. But is that all? Is it not much truer that ultimately it is not Jesus at all, but Pilate and the Roman state that are summoned before God's judgment seat, to be sentenced?

Jesus before Pilate, the procurator of the mighty Roman empire, brought there by the Sanhedrin, the authorities—that is to say, by the leaders of the Jewish people, those who made decisions in the name of the people, acted as their representatives. When John talks of "the Jews," we must think then of "the authorities," of the leaders who acted in the name of the people.

So, Jesus before Pilate. He had already been condemned but, according to Roman law, the Jews could not execute anyone. That could be ordered only by the lawful representative of the Roman state. Hence, on to Pontius Pilate, agent of the emperor.

John begins this episode with great irony and biting sarcasm. The high priests have brought Jesus to Pilate to be sentenced. But they do not go in, lest they should defile themselves. They are sure of their cases: "If he were not an evildoer, we would not have handed him over," they answer Pilate (18:30). "He calls himself the Son of God! He blasphemes!" They come with this purely *religious* charge to Pilate. Let it not be thought that the Sanhedrin was prejudiced! No, it submitted the matter to the neutrality and objectivity of the Roman government. Rome would not be prejudiced; it was famous for its neutrality!

But then, as soon as Pilate tries to slip out of the bothersome situation, it appears that after all there is more than just religion at stake: "If you free him, you are not Caesar's friend." And now comes the clincher: "Anyone who makes himself a king sets himself up against Caesar." And so, very subtly, the nature of the accusation against Jesus has been changed: Pilate is now being asked to render a *political* judgment.

We read later that he became afraid. What was taking place there between Pilate and Jesus, the prisoner from Galilee? How did it happen that the name of Pilate would for all time be associated with the suffering of Jesus Christ? John tries to show that Pilate was not concerned merely to get rid of the troublesome

Jew. It is also clear that he was not uninterested in the question of whether Jesus was guilty or not. He certainly was. We do not know the motives for his suddenly noble behavior, and in any case they are no longer particularly relevant. No, Pilate enters history with an ineradicable blot on his name because he approached Jesus with a feigned neutrality, both in his own stead and as a representative of the state.

"Do you say of your own accord that I am king?" asked Jesus.

"Don't ask *me* that question," Pilate says, "I'm not a Jew. I'm neutral! I just want to help you! Your own people handed you over; I didn't. I am merely asking. . . ."

But Pilate is already involved. Jesus *is* king. But his kingdom is not of this earth. The founding and source of his kingship are not of this earth, but of heaven. It comes to the earth, it comes to meet this earth; it is the future of the world.

This does not mean that there are no other kingdoms on earth, but it does mean that all other kingdoms, all other authority, will have to be measured against this kingdom of heaven. Every authority that pits itself against the authority of Jesus Christ must realize that from that moment its neutrality—or rather, its pseudo-neutrality—has been seen through, laid bare.

Jesus is also king in that he witnesses to the truth, and "everyone who is of the truth hears my voice." This is the responsibility that Christ himself lays on every individual and every political institution that has to deal with him. "Truth" is nothing other than the illuminating, liberating reality of God in this world, and this reality of God finds its expression in Jesus' association with *our* reality.

At the beginning of his work on earth Jesus described his mission:

> The Spirit of the Lord is upon me; therefore, he has anointed me to preach the good news to the poor, to proclaim liberty to captives, recovery of sight to the blind, and release to prisoners, to proclaim the acceptable year of the Lord [Luke 4: 18-19].

Indeed. And he did all this: ten lepers know it, and Zaccheus, and Mary Magdalene, and the adulterous woman in John 8, Nicodemus and Thomas and Peter, the Pharisees and the high priests, and now also . . . Pilate.

By asking "What is truth?" Pilate could not avoid God's word by resorting to philosophical argumentation, which might allow one to wash one's hands dramatically in "innocence" and carry on as if ultimately it is someone else's concern. In the end, there is no escaping one's responsibility.

Matthew throws light on this moment of truth in Pilate's life when he has him ask despairingly: "Then what am I to do with Jesus, who is called the Christ?" (Matt. 27:22).

When Pilate tries to avoid his responsibility in this way, both he and the government that he represents lose the legitimate ground on which they stand—because Pilate is called not only personally to hear the truth and act accordingly, but *in his personal hearing and in his personal decision the state itself is at stake.*

And because this was so with Pilate and the state he represented, he is delivered over to anxiety and intimidation: "And when Pilate heard that, he was the more afraid. . . ." And "if you release him, you are not Caesar's friend."

And "the Jews"? Again John's bitter irony: "And it was the day of preparation for the passover . . . and Pilate said to the Jews, 'Here is your king!' But they cried out, 'Away with him, away with him, crucify him!' 'Shall I crucify your king?' The chief priests answered, 'We have no king but Caesar.' "

At that tragic moment "the Jews" forfeited their messianic inheritance. And it was the day of preparation for the passover, when the remembrance of liberation from foreign subjugation would be celebrated, when God would be praised for their emancipation from the slavery of Egypt—the passover, when the omnipotence of the living God of Israel would be remembered over against the pharaoh's false claims to power, and when God's covenant with Israel, his chosen people, would also be commemorated.

Here there remains very little of that liberating memory. Just as little remains of the avowal and the joy of the psalmist:

> The Lord reigns; let the earth rejoice,
>   let the many islands be glad. . . .
> Righteousness and justice are the foundation of his throne.

. . . The heavens proclaim his righteousness,
and all peoples behold his glory.
All worshipers of images are put to shame,
who make their boast in worthless idols;
all gods are prostrate before him [Ps. 97].

The misled people, bewitched by the high priests and the authorities , trade the living God for the idolatrous Caesar, and thus deny God's sovereignty, the history of God's association with his people, *at the preparation for the passover.*

The people of God deliver themselves to the godless, demonic state, and the state hands Jesus over. The evil circle closes.

Nor do we escape our responsibility by saying that the gospel has no political consequences. We escape even less God's consuming judgment by acting as if we could remain neutral. As if we did not know the truth!

Because we know: neutrality is the most reprehensible partiality there is. It means choosing for those in power, choosing for injustice, without taking responsibility for it. It is the worst sort of politics, and the most detestable sort of "Christianity."

When the situation is as clear and unmistakable as it is with us, and when the cry of the poor and the wretched rises day and night to God, and injustice is there for everyone to see, then it is unforgivable for Christians to try to be neutral and apparently find it impossible to come down unequivocally on the side of right and justice. It is distressing that these things happen, that the NG [Dutch Reformed] Mission Church is a church that "stands in the middle," and that we are given a "special task of conciliation," instead of taking an outspoken stand for justice and liberation.

Black Christians who profess the lordship of Jesus the Messiah over their lives cannot with immunity bow before the worldly powers that deny God's love and trample his justice underfoot.

White South Africans cannot use fear as an excuse, or say that they feel constrained by the hatred that blacks might have for them. They must ask themselves to what extent the situation is what it is because they refused to hear and heed the voice of God's truth in their lives. Although it is late, hatred can still be avoided, if they even now will listen to God's voice.

We must realize that our reading of the passion obliges us to live the truth of God's liberating reality in our own lives and help to introduce it into the lives of others. It urges us to make of our history, in God's name, a history of liberation.

And what history is more liberating than the history of the crucified God?

Jesus before Pilate: the king, the way, the truth, the life. We have to choose for this Jesus, for his freedom, so that neither we nor our nation be delivered over to darkness and idolatry.

Those who will not choose for themselves will be doomed to the choices made by others.

3

Presence of the Hidden God

Faith; Doubt and Uncertainty; Hope

My soul thirsts for God, for the living God. When shall I come and behold the face of God? Why are you cast down, O my soul, and why are you disquieted within me? Hope in God, for I shall again praise him, my help and my God [Psalm 42].

Through him you have confidence in God, who raised him from the dead and gave him glory, so that your faith and confidence are in God [1 Peter 1:21].

Sometimes it seemed to me as though some wild beast had plunged his fangs into my heart, and was squeezing out its lifeblood. Then I began to question the existence of God, and to say: "If he does exist, is he just? If so, why does he suffer one race to oppress and enslave another, to rob them by unrighteous enactments of rights, which they hold most dear and sacred?" Sometimes I wished for the lawmakers what Nero wished: "That the Romans had but one neck." I

31

would be the man to sever the head from its shoulders.
Again said I: "Is there no God?"

These are the words of a black American bishop in the mid-
1800s. This is not a frivolous person speaking, a blasphemer who
recklessly pokes fun at God, but a man wrestling with his faith in
God in the same way as did the psalmist. Here God is not conven-
iently declared to be "dead," because he obstructs our human
plans and desires. No, here there is a serious and assiduous search
for God. Here is someone who knows that he cannot and does not
want to live without God, but who at the same time has a strong
feeling that God is no longer in his life, in his history, in his world
with its pain and desolation.

The psalmist also experiences this, which shows that the
bishop's question is as old as humankind itself.

The psalmist thinks of earlier times, when things were different. Then he was in the vanguard of jubilant crowds. Now he
stands alone. Earlier, things were better: "These things I remember, as I pour out my soul: how I went with the throng, and led
them in procession to the house of God, with glad shouts and
songs of thanksgiving."

Now he knows only the emptiness of despair, "as a hart longs
for flowing streams. . . ."

It seems that history is following its usual course, as if humans
were so powerful that they could give a decisive direction to history without God's being nearby . . . even worse, without any
need for God to be nearby! To the anxious question of believers
(and the mocking question of unbelievers): where is God? the
world answers: who is he? Belief in a provident God, who holds
his people in his hand and shapes world history according to his
will, seems a fortuitous relic of a more religious-minded age.

How are we to communicate to our contemporaries what faith
tells us about the course of our history? It cannot be demon-
strated with figures and statistics, and it cannot be calculated.
With a computer someone may be able to work out that we are
heading for disaster if we do not deal more intelligently with what
remains of our earth's natural resources. With the same certitude
we can work out for ourselves that race hatred in South Africa

will result in a large-scale bloodbath unless there is fundamental
change. Where does faith enter into this?

How Do We Experience God?

All too often our faith is powerless against human "superiority" —a humanity that thinks it is everything, that assumes sov-
ereign power. How are persons to experience God? Is he still a
reality for them?

In Colombia the son of a farm laborer—a squatter on a rich
man's estate, where people work and live like slaves, and eat mud
in winter to survive, and die of it—this youth said in answer to a
question: "God is the friend of generals and bishops, and he dines
with the landowner." In his experience God belonged with the
rich, with violence, with the "church." In his experience, they
were all the same.

How do persons experience God in their lives?

It is not a new problem: it seems to many that throughout history God has all too often appeared in the garb of the rich and the
privileged, standing on the side of the authorities and without
protest abiding by all the untruths, the half-truths, and the
equivocating myths. In South Africa God is white and he votes
for the Nationalist Party. Just as he blessed the weapons of the
Boer commandos a century and a half ago in the battle of Blood
River on Dingane's Day,[1] so today he blesses the weapons of the
riot police. And a clergyman who became a cabinet minister can
say without blushing: "To be an Afrikaner is to be white and
Afrikaans-speaking . . . on the side of right and justice, and on
the side of God."

Another matter: in Africa there are millions of persons who
have very little. And then comes a drought that destroys even the
little that they have. God, to whom the earth belongs, apparently
does not perceive their need. He does not send even a small cloud,
one "the size of a man's hand."

And yet again: in Soweto in 1976 anxiety and doubt exacted
their victims by the thousands and the call to God was an agonized
lamentation.[2] It was a year of affliction and what happened still
lies like an indigestible lump in our stomach.

We are back to our question of a moment ago. Can we still experience God? Because if we cannot any longer live in him by faith, then faith is devitalized and twisted into something unrecognizable.

But are things really as we have so far described? Must we therefore flee in despair from the world because God can no longer be found in it? I do not think so. The Bible teaches us that having faith in God is really to live in the world and in history.

Abraham learned this when, despite his advanced age, he believed God's word that his descendants would be like the stars of the heavens. It became clear when Israel pilgrimaged together with God in the exodus to meet a new future. It echoes in the prophecy of Isaiah that a remnant of God's people would return and become his people again.

It is a joyful message: God intervenes in our history, even intervenes *against* that history, when "the Word becomes flesh and lives among us." God's glory, his mercy, his involvement with humankind, and his victory are embodied in Jesus the Messiah. There is a *new* liberation: for prostitutes and publicans, for the powerless and the weak. He is God—the *living* God—even unto the very death of Jesus Christ.

This is what causes the psalmist's exultation: the *living* God! This is the fundamental difference between Yahweh and the idols: *he* lives! He lives for his people, with his people. He lives in everything that concerns them. This is the living God who revealed himself in Jesus of Nazareth, and who raised him to life, as our text from Peter says, ". . . so that your faith and confidence are in God." Or better still: "so that your faith is at the same time your hope in God."

Here faith and hope are the same thing. This means at the very least that barriers must be crossed, the barriers of powerlessness, barriers to believing what can be accomplished, barriers placed around us by the powers that want to control our lives. Faith is certain that God is real, and our hope is the certainty that he will reveal his reality. This is the psalmist's hope: "Why are you downcast, O my soul, and why are you disquieted within me? Hope in God, for I shall again praise him, my help and my God."

"I believe in Jesus Christ who arose in our lives so that we might be free of prejudice and arrogance, of anxiety and hatred, and pursue his revolution on the way to his kingdom" (Dorothee Sölle).

Once again, does faith in God mean that we escape from this world? Hang-glide over the earth in a permanent coma of solitary piety? Surely not! It is faith itself that forbids us to emigrate from history. Faith makes the Christian someone who, within history, sides with God's intentions for his creation against the tyrants who, in their madness, want to destroy the earth and its inhabitants. Faith sees that God is the living one whose supremacy is final.

Faith is hope in God and his will to heal this world, to save humankind. Faith is the refusal to accept God's concealment as his last word. He indeed is a God who refuses to take our sins, our sluggishness, our selfishness, as the last word.

This does not mean that if we believe we shall suddenly understand the meaning of all things. Many puzzles remain. Just ask a Russian Christian whether he finds it understandable to be discriminated against—to have his child refused a scholarship—simply because of his religious beliefs.

Who can wipe out the horror of a child's death? Who understands why a person becomes ill and has to suffer? Who comprehends the doubt and uncertainty that eventually stifle faith itself?

Our experience of God's reality consists in this, that we allow ourselves to be taken up in the struggle for God and his kingdom in our history. This means that every day we take again the road to God's kingdom and his justice, that we constantly seek to erect signs of his kingdom in our lives.

It is only in this commitment to God and his deeds in our history that we can give body to our faith, which is simultaneously hope, in God.

"Why are you downcast, O my soul, and why are you disquieted within me? Hope in God, for I shall again praise him, my help and my God."

And so we come back to the psalmist, and thus also to our American bishop, because his faith put him at the service of God, and of hope, and of those with whom he stood in fellowship:

I shall lift up my voice to plead [the] cause [of the oppressed] against all the claims of his proud oppressor; and I shall do it not merely from the sympathy that man feels toward suffering man, but because God, *the living God,* whom I dare not disobey, has commanded me to open my mouth for the dumb, and to plead the cause of the oppressed.

There *is* hope, because God is there, and—*thank God!*—so are we.

4

In the Wind and Fire

Pentecost

*When the day of Pentecost had come, they were all together
in one place. And suddenly a sound came from heaven like
the rush of a mighty wind. . . . And there appeared to them
tongues as of fire . . . resting on each one of them. And they
were all filled with the Holy Spirit [Acts 2:1–4].*

From time to time, diverse aspects of church doctrine and life
come to the fore. Emphasis shifts from one to another facet of the
Christian faith.

And so it is that today, throughout the world, the famous pentecost account has taken on fresh topicality—not so much because
of the central pentecost event, but because of what has been called
the "gift of tongues." This is because charisms—special gifts of
the Holy Spirit—are "in," and everywhere there is talk of a
"charismatic movement." This movement decries the "lifeless-
ness" of the Christian churches, including those in South Africa,
and wants to introduce Christians to the enlivening experience of
a new type of spirituality.

The movement has reached sizable proportions. Students are

coming to me with the question: are we really sure of our faith if we cannot speak in tongues?

A great danger with all our religious fads and fancies is that all too often we tend to interpret the Bible according to our own desires. For example, we make this pentecost text what *we* want it to be. And almost before we know what we are doing, we use the biblical narrative to force strange "heavenly languages" out of the throats of anxious Christians. Or, if they are unable to voice the right sounds, we make of their inability an impenetrable iron gate blocking the entrance to heaven.

Anyway, back to the text. The disciples are gathered in the upper room, anxiously awaiting a sign from the risen Lord. Perhaps it is better to say that they have shut themselves up in that room. Here they sit and talk, paying rapt attention to each other as they go over their recollections of their master. There is obviously a great danger that this little group could become an introverted sect.

And in this alone we glean the first important meaning of the miracle of pentecost: the pentecost story is about a crisis posed for all time by this little group. God fulfills his promise, the risen Lord keeps his word—and the church is born.

What happens now, at this very moment?

There comes, so we read, a sound like the rush of a mighty wind; the disciples see tongues as of fire; in one way or another those present are gripped, inspired, and they testify to it.

This testimony happens *in tongues.* We must not let ourselves be confused on this point. The languages spoken were not an incomprehensible babble resulting from a kind of swoon. The apostles were not so "transported" or "possessed" that they did not know what was happening to them at that moment. No, the only reference to such a thing ("they were full of sweet wine") is summarily dismissed by Peter.

But at that moment the Holy Spirit gave to this little group the ability to testify in all the languages then being spoken in Jerusalem. This meant that everyone would be able to understand. And the testimony was about the great deeds of God.

Hence the amazement of the bystanders: the Cretans and Arabs, the Parthians and Medes, the Mesopotamians and Judeans, and all the others—because "we hear them telling in our own tongues the mighty works of God" (vs. 11). This was a strange phenomenon, that complete strangers who did not know the others' languages were yet able to speak and be understood, thus giving rise to "amazement and perplexity" (vs. 12).

What all this means we can see in the sermon that Peter gave shortly thereafter. He showed that the events of that day had not simply fallen from the sky, but were the fulfillment of the explicit promise of God as expressed by the prophet Joel. This promise had now been kept. It was the God of Israel, the God of liberation, the God of the promise and of the covenant, who was at work here.

The wind and the fire were signs of his power and his presence, just as were the column of cloud and the column of fire in the past. The history of Yahweh's association with his people had not ended, but was confirmed in the person of Jesus of Nazareth. "This Jesus," Peter reminded those present, "you crucified and killed by the hands of lawless men" (Acts 2:23).

He was the Messiah, the one sent by God so that all would know that Yahweh was king and took an active part in the testing of his people. God it was also who called Jesus from the dead. With further quotations from the Psalms, Peter makes sure that his listeners understand that the liberating history of the God of Israel continues in the life and work of Jesus the Messiah. His Spirit is the breath, the power, the dynamism of God who renews and changes the world, who activates human resources. This is the Spirit, says Peter, "which you now see and hear" (vs. 33). The dominion and kingship of Jesus of Nazareth will be affirmed by the working of this Spirit.

"Let all the house of Israel therefore know assuredly that God has made him both Lord and Christ, this Jesus whom you crucified" (vs. 36).

This is what Peter says; it is clear, lucid, unambiguous. Herein lies the wonder: that humans, even persons such as Peter, are enabled by the power of the Holy Spirit to speak about the works of God—the liberating works of God—in such a way that everyone can understand. This is the language of a person filled with the Spirit.

Pentecost puts us in a different position—not only *now,* confronted by charismatic groups, but for a long time past. There is a tendency among many Christians to try to get pentecost into their grasp, to manipulate its content. But they strip it of its power; they deflect the sharp point of the gospel.

What does the pentecost narrative actually deal with? It is not about a language miracle in which Christians talk in nonexistent tongues while in a state of virtual physical collapse, and thus convince others of their possession by the Spirit. It is, rather, about the clear, direct language in which persons speak the name of Christ, the name through which alone salvation can come, the name above all other names. It is about a lucid, comprehensible language in which, without anxiety or false modesty, testimony is given to the involvement of the living God with his people today. It is about the clear language of the moving and vivifying Spirit who wills to change persons, to renew the world, and to prepare us for the kingship of the Messiah. Although crucified and killed by humans, and today still denied by them, he has been re-called from the dead by God himself.

Pentecost has to do with this sort of language, the kind of language used by Peter. And herein lies the wonder, that Christians in the world today can still speak this language of the Spirit.

This is a problem for Christians in South Africa. How many of us have the courage to give witness honestly and clearly to what the gospel exacts of us in this country? We are too afraid to say unequivocally that apartheid is sin, that it directly contravenes God's intentions for humankind. The dehumanization of black persons is justified by recourse to such formulas as "nuanced thinking" or, even worse, "Christian forebearance," while we remain silent—in *every* language—about the illness from which we, both black and white, are bleeding to death. And if there is any talking at all, it is frequently so circuitous and vague that it impresses no one—neither the government that needs admonishment, nor the tormented persons who need the sympathy and solidarity of the church.

How many of us in the Christian church stand silently by as other Christians who speak up for the oppressed—Steve Biko, Theo Kotze, Beyers Naudé, David Russel—are gagged as agitators and demagogues?

And so the prophetic witness of the church, the voice of the bride, becomes an inaudible, incomprehensible mumbling that makes no sense. And in our pulpits the roar of the lion in defense of justice (Amos) becomes instead nothing more than the pathetic squeak of a terrified mouse.

Once again, what is the pentecost story all about? Is it about the subtle or less than subtle manipulation of the pentecostal event, such as we have experienced it in the church's history? As, for example, in apartheid theology in which the tower of Babel rises up in importance above even the reconciliation offered in Christ? Some white theologians of repute are still earnestly assuring us that pentecost is in fact a confirmation of their theory of differentiation and separation based on the story of the tower of Babel. Here indeed the differences between peoples, their various languages (and thus also their habits, culture, and the like), are not obliterated by the Spirit, but in fact confirmed. "Each one heard them speaking *in their own language*" (Acts 2:6)[1] And so our racially separated churches are lent divine sanction and apartheid is held to be within the framework of the biblical message. In this way the story of pentecost is expounded, exploited, and extenuated.

Against this we repeat our clear and unambiguous *no!* We refuse to accept this heresy as gospel truth. The pentecost story deals with something utterly different. It deals with the confrontation between the power of the Holy Spirit and the power of sin in human life.

What happens when the Spirit takes possession of the lives of human beings? They begin to *move*. The stagnation and silence are broken through. Contentment with sin becomes unacceptable; discontent with wrong comes alive. The Spirit unerringly unmasks our complacency with evil and his word tears our hypocrisy to shreds. Religious nostalgia and other-worldly sighs give way to zest for the future, and strength is received for the search for repentance, the renewal of humankind and our world.

In brief, a church emerges. Community is born. Baptism takes place, bread is broken, and prayers are said in common. God turns things about and crumbles the harsh realities that hold us imprisoned: hatred, enmity, lovelessness, arrogance, and self-seeking. Reconciliation is fostered and solidarity turns to tangible acts of service. The members of the congregation care for each other, are concerned about each other, and live together from the power of the Spirit (Acts 4–5).

Here there is no place for separation and arrogance, no place for racial prejudice and hatred. Here there is no place for apartheid, whatever grand "Christian" name it may have attached to it.

The congregation filled with the Spirit testifies to all this, in the language of the Spirit, a language that *all* can understand and in which they can know and profess him.

"Let all the house of Israel therefore know assuredly that God has made him both Lord and Christ, this Jesus whom you crucified."

5

Like an Animal

Estrangement
Apropos of Soweto and Cape Town, 1979 [1]

The ox knows its owner, and the ass its master's crib; but Israel does not know, my people does not understand [Isaiah 1:3].

Bij de beesten af is one of those richly expressive Dutch idioms. It is always used in a negative sense, and by it is meant that someone's behavior or attitude is like that of an animal. When someone lives or acts in a way that reminds others of an animal, they are said to be *bij de beesten af*—like an animal.

Idioms are expressions of folk widsom; they reflect the inherited experience of living communities. They are accepted unquestioningly as "true" because their "truth" has been proven through communal experience. It is thus all the more interesting to see how the Bible here turns our folk wisdom upside down and, as it were, uses it against us. This is what is done here: Isaiah takes this idiom and he turns it about—it is not persons who are held up as examples against animals, but animals are used to shame persons. Through Isaiah's mouth God uses animals as examples for

43

us: "The ox knows its owner, and the ass its master's crib; but Israel does not know, my people does not understand."

The irony is bitter. An ox knows where to go when it is hungry, and even the stupid ass need not die of thirst, because it knows where to find its master's crib. But Israel, the people of God's love, the people to whom he has bound himself, with whom he established a covenant and forged a history, this people does not know. The implication is clear: they have no remedy for their hunger and thirst. They suffer and decline, because they no longer know where to go.

Bij de beesten af—like an animal.

The context in which all this occurs is also far from pleasant. Isaiah 1:1-9 describes the condition of the people as being like that of a desperately ill person, the result of a cruel and destructive war. Syria looms over the eastern world like a threatening cloud, and apparently we are also dealing with an invasion by Tiglathpileser and his armies that left behind them a trail of blood and destruction. Israel did not escape the slaughter.

Israel knows from experience not only the cruelty of the superpowers but also their incredible arrogance. Thus Hezekiah once had to listen to a message from Sennacherib, the king of Assyria, which makes it clear how cocksure the Syrians were of their superiority and how contemptuous they were of smaller nations:

Sennacherib, king of Assyria, sent his officials to Jerusalem with this message for King Hezekiah of Judah, and all the Judahites who were in Jerusalem: "King Sennacherib of Assyria has this to say: 'On what are you relying, while you remain under siege in Jerusalem? Has not Hezekiah deceived you, delivering you over to a death of famine and thirst, by his claim that "the Lord, our God, will save us from the grasp of the king of Assyria"? Has not this same Hezekiah removed his high places and altars [where idolatrous worship was offered] and commanded Judah and Jerusalem, "You shall prostrate yourselves before one altar only, and on it alone you shall offer incense"? Do you not know what my fathers and I have done to all the peoples of other lands? Were the gods of the nations in those lands able to save their lands from my hand? Who among all the gods of those nations which my fathers put under the ban was able to save his people from my hand? Will your god, then, be able to save you from my hand? Let not Hezekiah mislead you further and deceive you in any such way. Do not believe him! Since no other god of any other nation or kingdom has been able to save his people from my hand or the hands of my fathers, how much the less shall your god save you from my hand!" [2 Chron. 32:9–15].

Although the Lord had on that occasion intervened and saved Israel from the hand of Sennacherib, this time things went differently: Israel was flattened by Syria and the result was the sorrowful picture that Isaiah paints—a picture of blasted cities and razed villages, smoldering ruins and a bewildered, anxious people being relentlessly ground in the war machine. Nothing is left "whole." From the sole of the foot even to the head there was no soundness, but only "bruises and sores and bleeding wounds" that were "not pressed out, or bound up, or softened with oil" (Isa. 1:6).

And in verse 8 the prophet describes with compassion and poetic simplicity the total desolation and loneliness of the people: "And the daughter of Zion is left like a hut in a vineyard, like a shed in a cucumber field, like a beseiged city."

It is precisely this unnecessary loneliness that highlights both the condition of the people and the reason behind these terrible events. What of the assurance of God's nearness at all times and especially in times of affliction?

Did not this selfsame Isaiah—who here leaves the people standing utterly alone—witness to the God who would stay with them "when you pass through the waters . . . and through the rivers, they shall not overwhelm you" (Isa. 43:1)? Is not this nation the people of God's love, the people of his heart?

The mystery is immediately clarified when we read verse 4 again: "Ah! sinful nation, a people laden with iniquity, offspring of evildoers, children who deal corruptly! They have forsaken the Lord, they have despised the Holy One of Israel, they are utterly estranged."

There we have it. Here is the radical cause of the problem, and here is the reason for the grave condition of Israel. Hence the depiction in our text and the comparison with animals: Israel is estranged from Yahweh. It no longer knows its God. In a pronouncement of Judah and Jerusalem one would not now expect the name "Israel," which is a paraphrase for "the people of God," the congregation, the property of Yahweh, the nation of whom Yahweh again and again professed: "You are mine!" This makes the idiom of the ox and ass even more striking.

Our translation—"they are utterly estranged"—suggests a prolixity not in the original text, which is short and crisp: Israel does not know. Here *know* has the meaning of perceiving closely, noticing closely. It alludes to the alertness of someone who observes something extraordinary, like the woman who suddenly realized that the dead child in her bed was not her own: "when I look at it *closely* in the morning, behold, it was not the child that I had borne" (1 Kings 3:21).

But *know* also means to *recognize* and *acknowledge*. To recognize someone is to distinguish them from others; recognition is an acknowledgement of their otherness. Israel always knew that Yahweh was not like the gods of the heathen nations, but that he was indeed the Absolutely Other! Precisely because he is the Living One, ready to free his people, and precisely because he sets free the oppressed, acts justly toward the weak and the orphaned, toward the suffering and the poor, precisely for these reasons he is incomparable (Ps. 82). Israel learned to know him that way during the exodus and in the column of cloud and the column of fire, in the manna and in the water—in hunger and in thirst.

To recognize him as such; to acknowledge that it is he, still he; to acknowledge that he and he alone is God—this was what was lacking. Israel no longer knew him in this way. It had become estranged from him.

What is happening here is in direct conflict with the whole previous history of Yahweh and his people. It is the reverse of Exodus 3 where God reveals himself to Moses and then to his people as the Deliverer, and when he breaks pharaoh's power so that Israel can go free. It is also the reverse of what we read in Hosea: "When Israel was a child, I loved him, and out of Egypt I called my son" (11:1).

Israel is estranged from Yahweh. Something of this desperate inconceivability is to be found in the depiction of Israel by the prophet Jeremiah: "For my people have committed two evils; they have forsaken me, the fountain of living waters, and hewed out cisterns for themselves, broken cisterns, that can hold no water" (Jer. 2:13).

What followed speaks for itself. When there is estrangement from God, it is inevitably manifested in estrangement from one's human associates. In the Old Testament godlessness always meant neighborlessness. If God was no longer known and served, then the inevitable consequence was hatred, oppression, and anxiety. Then what was right was always twisted, the orphan and the widow found no help, justice became bitter wormwood, and the poor received less attention than the price of a pair of shoes.

The continuation of Isaiah Chapter 1 becomes a litany of suffering. Just listen:

> How the faithful city has become a harlot,
>   she that was full of justice!
> Righteousness lodged in her,
>   But now murderers.
> Your silver has become dross,
>   your wine mixed with water.
> Your princes are rebels
>   and companions of thieves.
> Everyone loves a bribe
>   and runs after gifts.
> They do not defend the fatherless,
>   and the widow's plea does not reach them [vs. 21–23].

Is it any wonder that Yahweh takes a dislike to their public worship? Considering their injustice and estrangement, can it be anything other than hypocrisy? Is it any wonder that what they call "worship" becomes for God an annoyance, "abominable perfumery"? I have had enough of burnt offerings of rams and the fat of fed beasts. . . . Your new moons and your appointed feasts my soul hates. . . . I will hide my eyes from you; even though you make many prayers, I will not listen: "your hands are full of blood" (vs. 11–15).

This is what happens when we turn our backs on God and our fellow humans, and then suddenly come face to face with the reflection of our own ugly image. Then even our worship is thrown back into our face like some rotten, putrefying thing.

The Spiral of Estrangement

In recent days many persons have come to me in dismay and desperation, and we have talked about what is happening in South Africa. Never before has such horror been so close to us. We all know what has been happening: how blacks, even children, in Bonteheuwel and Manenberg, in Bishop Lavis and Philippi, on the Parade in Cape Town and here in Bellville, blinded by tear gas, have been struck by bludgeons and gun barrels.

And there have been some newspaper reports that exceed even our worst suspicions—reports like the one on the man in Stellenbosch who was chased by the riot police into his own bathroom and there shot to death.

Many ask the question: how are such things possible? How can persons who are so "Christian" also be so brutal? There is, of course, an answer. At one level it lies in the fact that when persons defend a policy that in its essence is a denial of humanity, with the result that inhuman laws and views become "normal," then it is safely predictable that the defense of such a system will be just as inhuman. So it has been throughout history, with the defense of slavery and many other forms of oppression, and so it is still today.

At another level, however, the answer is to be found in the way that persons behave when they are estranged from God. Precisely for this reason apartheid is, in the final instance, sinful. The core of this policy is *estrangement*—aversion to one another, not seeing each other, not valuing each other. It is quite impossible to speak of reconciliation within the framework of this policy. Apartheid and its results are the appalling embodiment of estrangement from God and his Word. It is no wonder that South Africa looks the way it does.

We are estranged. From God and from each other. From our human destiny.

We are forced into a pattern of life that wants to make us believe that a person's right to be treated as a human being depends on the whiteness of their skin. Many of us believe that all our unhappiness would disappear if only we could have a larger slice of the capitalistic pie and not ask whether the advantages are derived from the suffering of others.

Whites are estranged from their own humanity. They cognitize themselves into the status of an idol and then see blacks not as human beings but as cogs in their economic machinery, servants in their homes, *things* with which a human relationship would be neither possible nor desirable.

And blacks are alienated from their own being, their own humanness. They have lived so long with their humanity undermined and unrecognized that they have to rediscover it for themselves before they can make any meaningful progress. For the black person, the white is not a fellow human but a *baas*—an enemy.

What we have here is an estrangement, an alienation, constrained to search everywhere for more victims.

Do you know what is the most striking thing about the story of the Good Samaritan? The fact that he did not need any law, any commission of inquiry, any synodal resolution, to do what was right and just.

There are those who say that we do not always know precisely what is right and just. The world is so complex, they say, and politics is the art of the possible. The prime minister frequently reminds us that the Bible is not a textbook in politics. Of course not! But then does the Bible really say nothing about human relationships, about right and wrong, about justice and injustice? Does God remain silent on these matters?

Were such arguments also the order of the day in the time of Micah and was the prophet confronted with rationalizations of injustice? It is striking how positive he is: "He has showed you, O man, what is good; and what does the Lord require of you but to do justice, and to love kindness, and to walk humbly with your God" (Mic. 6:8).

To know Yahweh is to know his will.

Even for our torn, alienated land there is still a chance. The familiar exhortation of Isaiah still applies:

Wash yourselves; make yourselves clean; remove the evil of your doing from before my eyes; cease to do evil, defend the

fatherless, plead for the widow. Come now, let us set things
right, says the Lord: though your sins are like scarlet, they
shall be as white as snow; though they are red like crimson,
they shall become white as wool [1:16–18].

Even for us there is still hope, because this same Yahweh can
also speak differently about Israel when it again learns how to
know him:

> In days to come,
> The mountain of the Lord's house
>   shall be established as the highest mountain
>   and raised above the hills.
> All nations shall stream toward it;
>   many peoples shall come and say:
> "Come, let us climb the Lord's mountain,
>   to the house of the God of Jacob,
> That he may instruct us in his ways,
>   and we may walk in his paths."
> For from Zion shall go forth instruction,
>   and the word of the Lord from Jerusalem.
> He shall judge between the nations,
>   and impose terms on many peoples.
> They shall beat their swords into plowshares
>   and their spears into pruning hooks;
> One nation shall not raise the sword against another,
>   nor shall they train for war again.
> O house of Jacob, come,
>   let us walk in the light of the Lord! [Isa. 2:2–5].

6

Resurrection and Insurrection

Easter

> *Let not sin therefore reign in your mortal bodies, to make you obey their passions. Do not yield your members to sin as instruments of wickedness, but yield yourselves to God as those who have been brought from death to life, and your members as instruments of righteousness [Romans 6: 12-13].*

It is noteworthy that in the Bible there is no theoretical argument for the resurrection of Christ Jesus from the dead. There is no minutely detailed logical reasoning—inductive or deductive—aimed at driving all counterarguments into the ground.

Even 1 Corinthians 15, which comes closest, is not really a theoretical argument, but much more a testimony of Paul's own faith. Moreover, the chapter ends with the only evidence that is either asked for or given in the Bible—namely, the life of the church itself:

> Therefore, my beloved brethren, be steadfast, immovable, always abounding in the work of the Lord, knowing that in the Lord your labor is not in vain (1 Cor. 15:58).

It is the same in Romans, in the chapter we have just read. In the final instance the matter revolves around the community and the manner in which the community of Jesus lives in the world.

"Let not sin reign in your mortal bodies," says Paul.

Here we need to be careful that our western education and thought patterns do not mislead us: for Paul, the Jew, there is no contradistinction between "body" and "soul." Too often we theologians, trying to help others to understand St. Paul, have explained his writings in a purely hellenistic way—that is, within a Greek philosophical context. We have too easily overlooked the fact that Paul, when all is said and done, remains a Jew, with a Jewish background, taught by Jewish rabbis, a man who clearly attempted to live according to the Scriptures—that is, the Old Testament. And so we must bear in mind that when Paul talks of the "body" he means the *whole person*.

Paul does not intend merely to emphasize certain "bodily," "steamy" sins—sex, gluttony, drunkenness; he refers rather to the sins of the whole human existence. Just as immoderate eating and drinking and the misuse of sex are sins, so too are abuse of power, exploitation, and avarice. So we must not understand the word "members" in verse 13 to refer to the sins of the hand, of the foot, of the eye, separately.

This reminds me of a little chorus that some of our children learn; it also imprinted an unbiblical distinction on my mind as a child:

> Be careful little hands, what you do . . .
> Be careful little eyes, what you see . . .
> Be careful little feet, where you walk . . .

What Paul has in mind is not specific, distinguishable parts, but "*any* part of your human existence."

In order then fully to grasp Paul's intention we need to translate our text thus: "Do not let sin reign in your earthly, human existence."

But there is something else we must bear in mind. Romans 6 also speaks of a struggle with sin: not so much the struggle between human nature and God, but the struggle between sin and God—or better still, between the dominion of sin and the dominion of lordship of God. Over against the dominion of sin stands the dominion of Christ. And so verse 12 can be read: do not let sin rule *as lord* in your earthly, human existence. That is to say, do not allow sin to take possession of you.

Dominion implies taking possession of; it means that one's thoughts and the whole of one's life are controlled. It demands total obedience and loyalty. Some persons are subjected to the power of destruction and inhumanity. Others are simply left to themselves, and this can be just as devastating.

Liberative Dominion

The lordship of Christ, however, is different. It is genuine, authentic power that does not force, intimidate, or threaten. The Messiah is Lord of humankind. His lordship liberates; it does not subdue or destroy. He gives life and his dominion brings justice and liberation, and spurs us on to serve God and our fellow humans. Sin exerts pressure abrasively; Christ stands at the door and knocks (Rev. 3:20).

Christians owe obedience and loyalty to Christ—an obedience that is not merely a talking point but a reality to be *lived* every day. This is why the distinction that Paul subsequently draws is so important: on the one side there is the inclination toward sin, on the other the inclination toward God:

> Do not yield your members to sin as instruments of wickedness, but yield yourselves to God as those who have been brought from death to life, and your members to God as instruments of righteousness (Rom. 1:13).

It is important to note that this distinction leads to what we emphasized at the beginning: the lifestyle of the Christian, resurrected community. It concerns service either to sin in the cause of injustice or to God in the cause of justice. Here there is no room for a patchwork faith with bits of this and bits of that.

Jesus the Messiah is on the way to his kingdom, and the resurrection-church may accompany him. Persons who have been enlivened by his resurrection are brought into action by his power and justice, which forms such an essential part of the lordship of

Christ and is of fundamental importance to them.

Such a church-community, alive through the resurrection of its Lord and with a faith that can correctly be regarded as a resurrection faith, can simply not tolerate injustice.

Such a church of the resurrection cannot regard crude exploitation of a people by a vulturous economic system as simply part of "our broken reality," about which nothing further is to be done.

The church of the resurrection cannot tolerate the wrong whereby parts of our country are "given" to certain groups by the rulers, so that other, rightless groups can be hounded out of them with a clear conscience.

The church of the resurrection does not know about "colored preference" areas, but only about a land given to us by God, in which there must be a home for *all* of us.

The church of the living Lord searches after justice and knows that the justice of his kingdom is not merely a philosophical exercise of arithmetic that gives "unto each his part." That becomes all too easy: to the good the good, to the bad the bad; to the capable the best, and to those less endowed the least. This kind of "achievement morality" is foreign to biblical justice.

The justice of the kingdom demands that the strong live for the weak and that they serve the weak. More: that they take up the cause of the weak against the powers that blindly oppress them and unscrupulously exploit their weakness.

We are churches of resurrection. We live in the certitude of the resurrection of Jesus Christ. And so do not let sin rule as king in your lives, because we have another king, a resurrected Messiah whose lordship stands fast. God has not only made him king, not only given him a name above all other names, but in the resurrection of Jesus God has finally broken the might of the last enemy.

The resurrection of Jesus Christ is God's insurrection against the eating away of our humanness, against the violation of his gospel, against the abominable misuse of his name in "Christian" South Africa. The resurrection of Jesus Christ is the insurrection, the rebellion of God against the Christian churches' compromise with the forces of evil. It is the revolt of the living God against evil.

What do we want of life?

Status, money, a degree, so that we may have "security"? Do

we want "repose"? Oh, especially repose—no more wrangling about squatter camps and migrant labor, no more whining about apartheid in the churches, no more ugly stories about starving children in the Ciskei—just repose.

Do we want a "good" future for ourselves—economic and political prospects, built on "colored preference"?

That is how the churches become henchmen of the devil! Instruments at the disposal of sin, vehicles of injustice. It is the intention of the gospel that things should be very different in the church of the resurrected Lord!

On Easter Sunday church members greet each other with the age-old, joyful profession: the Lord has risen! And with the certainty of faith comes the answer: Christ has *truly* risen!

Christ has truly risen! *We* are the only ones who can convince others that Christ has truly risen and that he lives in his church. Apart from us, there is no proof.

7

Do Not Be Afraid of Them

Anxiety
Apropos of Steve Biko

And do not fear those who kill the body but cannot kill the soul; rather fear him who can destroy both soul and body in hell [Matthew 10:28].

There is no fear in love; rather, perfect love casts out fear. For fear has to do with punishment, and he who fears is not perfected in love [1 John 4:18].

It is generally recognized that anxiety is one of the strongest factors that influence our behavior. Psychologists and behaviorists warn that anxiety is an unavoidable reality in the life of every person. Some maintain that anxiety is a kind of safety mechanism that automatically comes into operation when we feel threatened. Someone who claims never to be frightened can be very dangerous to associate with.

In any case, anxiety is a factor to be considered. The Bible considers it. The texts just quoted have to do with it.

We all have our large and our small anxieties: things that nag at us, things that annoy, that sometimes keep us awake at night. We are all afraid of war—a race war—that could erupt in this subcontinent; in its destructive hatred and lunacy perhaps no one would be spared. We hear of a horrendous atomic threat that could result in an explosion that would wipe out large parts of our world without a trace.

But that is a little remote: anxiety is more of a problem when it acquires a face, when it becomes tangible, and we cannot get out of its way, when it takes on the recognizable features of a human countenance.

Jesus speaks about this in our text. In calm, objective tones he talks specifically about anxiety. He says plainly that those who follow him will experience moments of acute anxiety in their lives. And for him, too, anxiety has a name: "Be on your guard with respect to others; they will hale you into court . . ." (Matt. 10:17). Jesus knows what is going to happen. He knows what *must* happen if his followers are going to proclaim the gospel to the world. He knows there will be opposition to his message, which runs counter to so many human tendencies. He knows of the intransigence of a world that does not want to know anything about the gospel of the kingdom.

But notice the context: the disciples receive from Jesus the command to go and proclaim the gospel. Both to those who wish to hear and to those who shut their ears they must profess Jesus Christ as Lord and king. They must carry forward the work begun by him. Notice that despite all the warning about the obvious dangers attached to this discipleship and the obvious risks that will have to be taken, Jesus never revokes his command. On the contrary.

With whom is Jesus talking here? Certainly not with "superheroes," who would seem unreal to us, but with persons whom we all know of, quite ordinary persons: Simon Peter who would later betray him, his brother Andrew, Matthew the tax collector, and Simon the Zealot, freedom fighter and guerrilla. Judas Iscariot is also there. Each of them is a reflection of the church's membership today, persons with weaknesses and problems, quite ordinary persons.

They knew what it was to be afraid. They formed part of a nation that was bowed under the Roman yoke. They never knew if they would still be alive on the morrow.

How many of them happened to be on hand when the Zealots (the Jewish freedom fighters who lived in Galilee) decided to attack Roman soldiers or when Pilate's arrogance evoked an enraged reaction from the people? Were they not afraid to say the wrong things, or let an incautious word fall from their lips? After all, they never knew when there was an eavesdropper or government informer in the vicinity. Considering the ruthlessness of Pontius Pilate who did not hestitate to pursue rebellious Galileans even into the temple and then murder them (Luke 13:1-5), it is clear that they knew what it was to be afraid.

But this was not all. Besides the political oppression of the Romans, there was also the religious tyranny of the Pharisees and scribes. They made of the Torah of God—the law—a burden and a heavy rock, crushing believers with its inflexibility, instead of what God had intended, a plan to directive injunctions based on liberation. They throttled the simple people with their religiosity and their numerous little commandments and prohibitions that completely soured the joy of the law about which Psalm 119 speaks. In the words of Jesus, in their fanaticism they "shut the doors of the kingdom of heaven in others' faces" (Matt. 23:13). The worship of Yahweh, which should be an exhilarating, liberating experience, had become an oppressive, suffocating fustiness. The disciples themselves had to live under this tyranny of piety before they came to know Jesus.

These were the persons with whom Jesus spoke, and this was the real-life context in which his words reached them. Persons without fame or status, without protection or security, delivered over to the forces that set the tone in their world.

What is more, it is Jesus who speaks. He too knew what anxiety and suffering are! He too knew moments of anquish and utter despair so that he was forced not only to pray, "Take this cup from my lips," but also "My God, my God, why have you forsaken me?" His path was to lead to Gethsemane, and through Gethsemane to Gabbatha and Golgotha.

That is why he did not try to soothe or rationalize away the anxiety of his disciples. He also did not attempt cheap words of comfort in the spirit of "just believe in me and nothing will happen to you" or "that simply happens to be a disciple's fate."

He held out something else for himself and his disciples. He took their anxiety seriously and offered something else in its place: fear of the Lord.

"Do not fear those who kill the body but cannot kill the soul: rather fear him who can destroy both soul and body in hell."

At first this sounds extraordinary! Does Jesus want to remove his followers' fear by putting a greater fear in its place? Fear of hell, in fact? The original Greek was quite clear: people can kill, but God can destroy—so that literally nothing would remain. Was this merely a clever psychological ploy that Jesus was using against the disciples?

Certainly not, because the phrase "fear of the Lord" is a common one in the Old Testament, and Jesus, standing as he does squarely within the tradition of the Torah and the prophets, wants this old truth to live again for his followers.

The "fear of Yahweh" is fundamentally different from the panicky anxiety, the trepidation, or even terror that human beings can bring about; it is an alternative fear that effectively displaces and excludes fear of human beings.

This greater fear finds expression in faith in him, in trust in him, and in obedience to him. *Belief* in him rather than in idols that cannot see, hear, and liberate. *Trust* in him instead of in human plans and systems that are inwardly rotten and infected by sin unto death itself and on account of their injustice bound to disappear. *Obedience* to him and his word instead of a blind servility that distorts reality and leads to the precipice. Those who wish to imitate Jesus the Messiah in the world are required so to believe in him that the anxiety in their lives is overcome.

There must be a reason why oppressors are always afraid. They know that to retain their privileged positions and to maintain the existing power structures they will have to use ever more violence. There is thus always a vicious cycle of oppression, hatred, anxiety, and violence. The oppression causes hatred on the part of the oppressed, and a longing to be free, which in its turn creates anxiety in the oppressor that he will have to surrender his privileges. To prevent this, he uses more violence in the attempt to secure this position. The greater the violence, the greater the danger of counterviolence by the oppressed who yearn to be free. Eventually the whole vicious cycle becomes a descending spiral.

We have said that anxiety is an unavoidable factor in the life of every person. We too are not free of it. How fast we cling to old, played-out ecclesiastical forms and worthless rituals that stand in the way of our liberation! Why? Not so much because we really want to retain these things but because we cannot overcome our fear of change.

If we look deeply and honestly into our own hearts we shall have to admit that we have a deep-rooted fear of our own liberation. Once we have been converted, once we know that God has freed us in Jesus Christ, once we have confessed Jesus as king and accepted his word as our guide, then we have to live accordingly. Then we shall have to evince what Calvin said so long ago: "Christians always have to be in a certain sense disturbers of the established order, because they have to point out, explicitly or implicitly, the unfairness and injustice of the society in which they find themselves, while they seriously take up the Word of God and live according to it."

This is in fact what is expected of liberated persons, and we shall not be able to evade it.

Love vs. Fear

Steve Biko's death in a prison cell brings the fear in our own hearts oppressively to the fore. It is an exacting task to remain loyal to Christ. To remain obedient to him is very dangerous. Yet for Christians obedience to Christ and his word comes first, and certainly before obedience to government officials. For this reason the Christian Institute's struggle is very important for Christians and for the church in South Africa. The central issue in the life of this little group of Christians concerns expression of and witness to this evangelical demand: obedience to the word of God, and loyalty to the Messiah, which are greater than fear of other persons.

Our text from St. John draws our attention to something else; love drives out fear. This is the love that Jesus refused to relinquish and that enabled him to keep on to the end. It is this love that nurtures obedience and leads to liberation.

Love stands diametrically opposed to fear. Love frees, fear confines. Love creates space for others, knows commitment to others, allows others to grow to full humanity. Fear drives others away, makes persons artificial. Love binds and searches for genuine peace; it neutralizes hatred. Fear sows hatred and intolerance, causes distrust and suspicion, estranges, and undermines our humanity.

We need to ask ourselves not only whence our fear comes, but also where we lost our love.

What we are experiencing today in South Africa—the unexplained deaths of so many persons held in detention, the meddling with persons' private lives, the crescendoing violence, the recourse to yet more repressive legislation—is the precipitation of unreasoning fear, and thus the apex of inhumanity.

The only genuine answer is the love that seeks peace and justice, the love that can drive out fear.

And this love is not sickly sentimental, does not paper over sin, but searches openly, honestly, and actively for justice and rejoices in it (1 Cor. 13).

Behind the fear of a race war is a yet greater fear, that of loss of position and of sharing privileges. Behind the fear of "communism" is the fear that the church's involvement in oppression will be unmasked. It is tragic, but true: the church of Jesus Christ in white South Africa and in the rich countries is no longer the sheep sent in among the wolves; it itself behaves all too often like a wolf against the poor and the voiceless.

Behind the fear of the "agitator" is a deep fear of justice. Persons are bought over with counterfeit justice, with superficial adaptations aimed at consolidating the status quo, because behind the fear of justice is a fear of change itself.

As the church of Jesus Christ we shall have to choose between fear and love.

In all these conflicts the faithful may yet hold fast to the words: "To me is given all power in heaven and on earth. . . . And see, I am with you unto the very ending of the world." His power is a loving power that does not destroy but liberates, does not threaten but frees. In our activity in the world in his name, may we realize that his power is the critical yardstick against which all powers and all authorities on this earth will ultimately be measured.

We are involved with Christ in history and amid all the events of our time we must go our way with him. This means that we shall have constantly to choose: for him and against all rebellions against Christ and his dominion, even if the rebellion is carried out by the established order; for him and against all demonry that attempts to destroy justice and give love no opportunity, even if this demonry should be camouflaged in a cassock; for him and against all fear which holds back the conversion and renewal of God's world, even if that fear appears in the form of a gun or a torture cell.

So fear not those who can kill the body but not the soul. Rather fear him who can destroy both body and soul in hell. . . . And remember: "Everyone who acknowledges me before others, I will also acknowledge before my Father in heaven; but whoever denies me before others, I will also deny before my Father in heaven." And: "All authority in heaven and on earth has been given to me . . . and lo, I am with you always, to the ending of the world."

8

The Law of Christ

Reconciliation and Forgiveness

Bear one another's burdens, and so fulfill the law of Christ [Galatians 6:2].

The names of some evangelical ideals are today treated with suspicion, because of years of facile misuse. Reconciliation and forgiveness—essential in the lives of Christians and Christian congregations—are examples of it. There are many black Christians who frown when someone talks of reconciliation—not so much because reconciliation is regarded as unnecessary but because "reconciliation," "forgiveness," "love" are words that have been glibly used by "Christian" authorities to frustrate opposition and protest.

And yet the church of the Lord cannot afford to live without these words and what they symbolize. Readiness to accept forgiveness and reconciliation is an evangelical precondition for a whole, Christian life. The parable of the uncharitable creditors (Matt. 18) is not in the Bible for nothing, and the urgency with which Paul asks the Corinthians, "We pray you, for Christ's sake, to reconcile yourselves with God," has today lost none of its urgency.

The reality of that time—partisanship, distrust, suspicion, prejudice—is still present in the Christian churches and if the apostle were to write a letter to them today he would surely use the same words: "Bear one another's burdens, and so fulfill the law of Christ."

In its own way, this is a kind of summary of Christian morality. As such, it is all-inclusive and unchangeable. By the same token, it is a rock that the Christian church dashes itself against, time and again. It is here that the church's obedience is tested. It is here that it can be seen whether we are prepared to follow Jesus and, accepting the fact that he is on our side, show that we are on his side.

It is strange that Paul speaks of a "law." What does this mean? Is it not also in this letter to this same congregation that Paul argues against a slavish adherence to the law, against legalism? The whole of chapter three and four deals with this theme of freedom from the law, and chapter five begins with Paul's famous cry of triumph: "For freedom Christ has set us free; stand fast therefore, and do not submit again to a yoke of slavery."

So when he now goes on to speak of a "law," it is clear that it—this "law of Christ"—is essentially different from the legalism he has just been warning against. The fact that it is unchangeable is another difference.

First of all it seems that Paul's choice of words is intended to remind us of the spirit and tone of the Ten Commandments in Exodus 20: injunction—"you shall (not) . . ."—and fulfillment of the law are paired. The same coupling is made in the Pauline text. In other words, Paul does not suggest that the Christian community has a choice of whether it wishes to observe this law or not—if you are a church of Jesus Christ, this is not a matter for discussion. Professing to be a church of the Messiah makes fulfillment of the law of Christ a necessity. And indeed we are the church of *Christ!*

Besides—and here we come to another correspondence with the Ten Commandments in Exodus 20—Christ himself gave this law of his a clear content in two memorable statements in Matthew 11:28-30:

Come to me, all who labor and are heavy laden, and I will give you rest. Take my yoke upon you, and learn from me;

for I am gentle and lowly in heart, and you will find rest for
your souls, for my yoke is easy, and my burden is light.

This "yoke of Jesus," the burden of which he speaks, is none
other than the "law of Christ" to which Paul refers. Jesus makes
two very important matters clear to us: first, and once again, the
correspondence with the law of Exodus 20—namely, that both
laws fall within the framework of liberation. The "space of
freedom" that Yahweh created for his people through liberation is
the background to the Ten Commandments. The law begins with
it—"I, the Lord, am your God, who brought you out of the land
of Egypt, that place of slavery" (Exod. 20:2)—and in its light we
must read and understand the necessity for obedience.

Precisely because this people has been freed from the yoke of
the pharaoh, precisely because the oppressive power of slavery
has given way to the liberating and re-creating power of the right-
eous God, precisely because this space to know and hear him, to
follow him, is now theirs—precisely for these reasons the people
can be expected to use their new freedom to serve the Living One.

We find the same thing in the law of Christ: it is framed by the
reality, the mercy, the love of the Messiah himself. His life's work,
his obedience, his liberative deeds are the content, the force, and
the fullness of his law. The joyful truth of the Torah, and the joy
over the differentness of this law, lies in the undertone: the liberator is the lawgiver.

A second, no less vital, consequence flows from this. In our
text the law is called "the law of Christ." And indeed it *is* his law;
he enacted it and he carried it out. It was he who was willing to be
the mediator between God and humankind. It was he who
through his passion and death became the reconciler, the agent of
God's salvation for humankind. For the sake of humankind he
became the bearer of a great burden: in his death on the cross he
bears the sins of the world, our indolence, our unwillingness, our
selfishness. He bears the weight of the terrible estrangement between God and ourselves, and between us and our fellow humans.
And this path led him through the bitterness of the struggle in
Gethsemane to the cross of Golgotha.

Reconciliation with God and among humans exacts a price,
and the community of the reconciled cannot expect anything else.

In this way also Christ becomes our liberator, and the liberator is the lawgiver. Whoever believes in the liberation of humankind through the Messiah cannot bypass his law. And whoever obediently executes the law discovers that it is the law of the liberator. For this reason Jesus calls his yoke easy and his burden light. And obedience to this law leads to "rest for the soul."

So we come now to the law itself. "Bear one another's burdens." It should be clear that Paul is not pleading here for "tolerance." He is not asking for a forbearing society (a call often heard today). There is no question here of a superficial forbearance allowing everyone to be left "to themselves and their own judgment." The apostle is asking the members of the Christian community to carry each other's burdens—to carry each other.

Naturally we each have our own burdens that have to be carried, and the Bible accepts this. In fact, Paul himself refers to this a few verses later on. And who of us does not know it? The things about ourselves with which we constantly wrestle: the secret, private sins that make it impossible for us to allow God to be God in our lives and to accept our fellow humans in true fellowship. Who of us does not know the feelings of impotence and frustration that attack us because we can see what is wrong with our society, because we know of the injustices perpetrated day after day, because we so greatly wish to demonstrate our solidarity with others but cannot—because the system is a monstrosity that brooks no opposition? We know these things, and they are burdens we are forced to carry—day in, day out.

"The Others"

But in our text the apostle has something else in mind. Responsibility for the *other,* the burdens of the *other:* these we must bear. We have to learn to see the other, him or her. As Christians in the real world we are not confronted with mere "cases" or abstractions, but with persons, with fellow beings for whom the gospel places an obligation on us. We are called to bear one another's burdens—those burdens of sin that, whether subtly or blatantly pleading for our help or spurning it, bow the backs of our fellow humans.

This applies to those in our society who have even less than we

do, our black brothers and sisters. It applies to those persons
who, even though they are just as suppressed as we are, fall into
an even lower socio-economic category. They are the "others"
who constantly direct an appeal to me, and whose inability to
express their anxieties and longings lays the responsibility on me
to do so in their stead, and to struggle for their right without
compromise or cessation. Those who wish to be of the community
of Christ cannot do otherwise: they must "bear one another's burdens."

But this law pertains not only to those who rely on me and who
depend on my solidarity, it applies also to those who do not arouse
my compassion but my repugnance. The oppressor, the government official who remorselessly uses his power to give me a
second- or third-rate status so that my "citizenship" in my country of birth is merely an empty label. The exploiter, degrading me
to the level of a cog in his economic machine, underpaying me so
that his profits and his social position may be safeguarded. The
political manipulator thinking up noble-sounding names for his
inhuman laws and with breathtaking arrogance even calling them
"Christian." All these are included in "the others." They too
come within the purview of the law: Bear one another's burdens.
The root of the matter is that their pride, the injustice that they
perpetrate, the self-serving attitudes that they display, the apartheid that they practice—all these are sin—signs of their estrangement from God and from me. Bear their burdens! Because solidarity, forgiveness, and reconciliation cannot be ignored. Those
who wish to be of Christ's assembly have no option: "Bear one
another's burdens."

Here we are called to an obedience and an emulation that cannot be evaded. We may not attempt to rationalize away our responsibility, or hide behind our (justified) political prejudices.
Forgiveness and reconciliation are too real for that, and the demands of the gospel too clear-cut. We may not attempt to play the
part of God; those who wish to be of the congregation of Christ
have to make his commandment their own. We have to take this
seriously, because the price that Jesus Christ paid was too high to
be worthy of anything else.

For this very reason we have to take care that we do not participate in the familiar and dangerous sport in which reconciliation

and forgiveness are abused. Prepared to exercise forgiveness and reconciliation? Reconciliation cost Jesus Christ his life; it demands its price. To live together reconciled as black and white in this country is a function of grace, and grace always makes demands. Reconciliation will never become a reality without confrontation, without paying the price. Forgiveness does not mean that sins are simply covered over; reconciliation is not the deft, or pious, concealment of guilt. On the contrary! Reconciliation follows upon the exposure, the unmasking, of sin.

Too long have Christians in this country attempted to avoid genuine reconciliation by proclaiming a "unification" that rests on a cloaking of guilt and on a pious silence about evil. Too long have they tried to achieve reconciliation through apartheid, as if the two did not stand diametrically opposed to each other. Let us be honest about this: reconciliation is not holding hands and singing "Black and White Together." Reconciliation is not blacks and whites going to summer camp together. Reconciliation is not holding a "multi-racial" South African Christian Leadership Assembly where we set aside apartheid and live in fellowship "in the Spirit" for a month, and then return to our separate and separated lifestyles. Reconciliation is not merely "feeling good" but *doing what is right*. And only when this is the issue for the South African Christian Leadership Assembly can success be expected.

Besides, reconciliation does not occur between "whites" and "nonwhites," or between ruler and ruled. Genuine reconciliation does not occur between oppressor and oppressed—it occurs between persons, persons who face each other in their authentic, vulnerable, and yet hopeful humanity. And therefore liberation, complete with total liberation of human beings, is inevitably bound up with reconciliation. And with forgiveness.

Forgiveness of guilt is preceded by confession of guilt. As long as white Christian South Africa will not acknowledge its collective guilt and will not confess it, as long as Christians are anxiously exhorted not to have feelings of guilt, so long will the evil that keeps us unreconciled also remain unlanced and unhealed.

The dictum remains: "Bear one another's burdens, and so fulfill the law of Christ." If black Christians in South Africa disregard this truth, if we try to deny its reality in our lives, if we try to manipulate the gospel on this point, then we are not worthy of the

name Christian. And if we make reconciliation something superficial and forgiveness something cheap then the judgment of God
will strike us. The blood of Jesus Christ is too precious for that,
and the blood of his martyrs too precious in his eyes.

But the yearning remains. The church of Christ longs for reconciliation and searches for it. In reconciliation Christ breaks open
the demonic realities that imprison our lives: the anxiety, prejudice, hidden pride, lust for power, desire for vengeance. Our humanity is addressed and placed in God's presence through confession of guilt and forgiveness of guilt.

In conclusion, two more points:

"If you do not forgive others, neither will your Father forgive
you" (Matt. 6:15).

"The whole law has found its fulfillment in this one saying:
'You shall love your neighbor as yourself' " (Gal. 5:14).

This is how God's word expresses it. Is there anyone who wants
to say it differently?

9

The Eye of the Needle

Eligibility for Entrance into the Kingdom

> *They were bringing their little children to him to have him touch them, but the disciples were scolding them for this. Jesus became indignant when he noticed it and said to them: "Let the children come to me and do not hinder them. It is to just such as these that the kingdom of God belongs. I assure you that whoever does not accept the reign of God like a child shall not take part in it" [Mark 10:13–15].*

Our text is a "foreign incursion" into the cohesion of Mark chapter 10. There is no obvious connection with the context. There is no obvious thread running through the chapter. What precedes it and what follows is something entirely different from what is discussed in our text. But perhaps that was precisely the intention, so that what we are offered in verses 13 to 16 would stand out all the more clearly. It is as if Mark draws a red circle around this section so as to direct his reader's attention to it with special emphasis. Consequently, verses 13 to 16 leap to the forefront of the chapter, as it were. And that is good, because they are of vital significance.

We need not follow the drawn-out debate of some commen-

taries concerned with whether it is with infants or older children
that we have to do here. The argument is, I feel, not essential to
the passage. The fact is that mothers are bringing their children to
Jesus so that he would bless them.

It probably has to do with an old and charming custom: parents
were keen to bring their children to a celebrated rabbi for his
blessing. The fame of the man from Nazareth, with his authorita-
tive way of saying things, his way with the people, and his deeds
preceded him. He too is petitioned to "lay his hands" on the
children. . . .

At this point the disciples consider that they have reason to
intercept these parents and their children. They do not think it
right for the people to take up Jesus' time like this. The exact
reason for their action is not given by the evangelist, and we do
not want to succumb to the temptation of indulging in specula-
tions as to why it happened. The reason will, I think, presently
become clear when we deal with Jesus' reaction.

In Mark's version Jesus' reaction is especially severe. Matthew
and Luke allow Jesus to speak directly to the children without
mentioning whether anything else occurs. But in Mark as on other
occasions, the reader is also told what Jesus is thinking at that
moment. Our Afrikaans translation, "He took great exception to
it," and most English translations, "he became indignant," or the
equivalent, are very mild. The language Mark uses is much
stronger. According to Mark, Jesus was furious with his disciples.
A literal translation goes something like: *he was boiling inside.*
What follows is thus not said in tones of gentle reprimand, but
with deep and strong feeling and anger: "Let the children come to
me and do not hinder them. It is to just such as these that the
kingdom of God belongs."

A number of things are made clear here to the attentive reader.
Jesus' reaction stems from the same source as the reaction of the
disciples a short while before, when they wanted to keep the little
children away from the Messiah. To understand correctly their
action, as well as the words and attitude of Jesus, we must delve a
little deeper, in particular into the position of the child among the
Jews that time.

There is no question that the child was not seen as God's child,
as such. On the contrary, the child was the very model of unim-

portance, of those who were not to be considered. The romantic image of the child that has grown in our pietistic tradition and that we have subsequently imported into our religious life is distinctly un-Jewish. The child was not seen as the model of purity and innocence. Rather, the child stood more or less on a par with those who counted for nothing, those peripheral to the real world, the good life; they were the "little people" who could claim no status at all.

If Jesus promises the kingdom to these children who are blocked by the disciples for precisely this reason—after all, on what grounds do they have the right to see the master?—he does not do it on the basis of any special quality that these children possess: childlike simplicity, trust, innocence, or open-mindedness. On the contrary, he makes it known that the kingdom of God is destined for the nobodies, the despised, the unimportant ones!

And herein lies the proof of the radicalism of the kingdom of God. The Messiah makes it plain that his realm is not intended for the prominent, the rich, the status-holders, the powerful; no, quite the reverse! What verse 15 says is: those who do not grasp this truth and take it to heart and govern their lives in accordance with it shall not enter the kingdom of God.

This nettling attitude of Jesus has not been digested by the church even today. And the antics performed to circumvent it are strange to behold. Then as now, this attitude of the Messiah (which, incidentally, is maintained consistently throughout the whole Bible) stands at odds not only with what the "world" wants, but also with what the church wants!

The Paradoxical Kingdom

Jesus here announces, for the umpteenth time, the inverted order of the kingdom of God. What prevails in the kingdom runs counter to the way we would have preferred it. Here the first are last, and the last first. In the kingdom of God, it is not the powerful who, because of their power, walk off with the spoils; the powerful are those who have compassion on the weak and who use their strength to right the wrongs that plague the weak. It is not the wise who are chosen, on account of their wisdom; God uses the fool to shame the wise. If we, the church of Jesus Christ, do not understand this, we will not enter the kingdom of God because our style of doing things is precisely the reverse.

In the church we favor and adulate the rich and influential; the unimportant and poor must take a back seat. We look differently at them, we talk differently to them. Evangelism is conducted in the poor neighborhoods, not in the suburbs where large cars stand before the doors. In the church we meekly and profusely thank the rich who out of their abundance give to the Lord (even though it is less than they squander in one night), but the poor widow, and the family with a jobless father, who give out of their poverty and uprightness, we do not notice.

All too often we have a double standard for applying discipline. The esteemed of the community and their children are shielded from reprimand by all manner of adroitness, but the others, the insignificant ones, get no privileges. But, says Jesus, the kingdom of heaven belongs to them. And if we do not understand this, we shall not enter the kingdom of God.

It *is* difficult to comprehend. The kingdom, and the God of this kingdom, are not pinned down by *our* definitions and *our* concepts. Nor is God obligated by our ethical norms, though we think that we have extracted these norms from the Bible. Christians sometimes advance a theory of "tolerance" that is in fact alien to the Bible. In contradistinction to our pious nuances, the God of the Bible is partial. He takes sides. He chooses for Israel against the pharaoh; for the oppressed against the oppressor. We might then say: "How sad for the pharaoh," or "What about the oppressor?" But if oppressors do not understand and do not change their lives accordingly, then they too will not enter the kingdom of God.

There is nothing to be done about it; this is the way the God of the Bible is: he dethrones the powerful and elevates the humble. He fills the hungry with good things and sends the rich away empty-handed (Luke 2:52–53).

The witness of the Bible is clear. This is the God of Israel; he restores the oppressed to justice and he confuses the path of the godless (Ps. 146). And if the rich and the powerful do not comprehend this, they will not enter the kingdom of God. Because in the church we wish to think and speak with "nuances," we allow to stand in harmony those whom the Bible places *opposite* each other. We want oppressors to remain and to be reconciled with the oppressed. We are disinclined to make the *broederbonder* choose between his secret loyalty and his brotherhood in Christ.[1]

We dare not be more Christian than is the Bible. The church of Christ will have to prove, in its life and in its witness, that it understands this word of its Lord, and that it has made it its aim. If the community of the Messiah is thereby made vulnerable, if we thereby lose the wealth and power we possess, if we thereby disturb the anxious peace that we keep with the powers that be, then the consolation of the gospel is that we shall sooner enter the kingdom of God without these things than with them.

"Hinder Them Not"

There is one thing left that requires our attention. The disciples crowd around Jesus so closely that the mothers are unable to approach him. Here we are arrested by the remarkable phrase of Jesus: "Hinder them not. . . ." Here we are not asked to *bring* the children (however important that too might be); we are simply asked *not* to *hinder* them. In this expression of Jesus, in which he ostensibly asks for so little, lies, in my view, a criticism that cuts deeply. It is a scathing indictment of us. It is apparently much more typical of us to keep children away from Jesus!

It could be that the church, with all good intentions, is holding up an image of Jesus to our children that repels rather than attracts them. The Jesus whom the church announces is often nothing more than the product of an anemic theology, a Jesus *so* far removed from the pressures and the reality of contemporary lives that his word passes them by without leaving a trace.

There is a further possibility: that the church shows so few characteristics of what a church ought to be, demonstrates so little of the unity of faith, of the quest for justice, of hope and love, of solidarity and reconciliation, that these absences ultimately become a wall behind which Jesus becomes invisible, or inaccessible, to the world and to our children. "Hinder them not. . . ."

When we think of the role that black children are playing in South Africa today, of their involvement in the politics of change, of their willingness—on the basis of their faith—to sacrifice everything for the sake of human liberation, these words of Jesus become even more charged with meaning and urgency. It is when we see them marching in the streets, risking their futures, willing to lay down their lives—indeed, when we see them dying on our streets—for the sake of a renewed South Africa, that we understand anew the words of Jesus: "It is to just such as these that the kingdom of God belongs."

To make it all clear, Jesus suffers the little children to come to him, and he blesses them. So doing, he demonstrates that the kingdom, that priceless treasure, is intended precisely for them. He does not judge them too unimportant or insignificant, because they are unable to grasp the depth and richness of this secret.

To comprehend and carry out the depth and extent of this radicalism of the gospel is to earn the right to inherit the kingdom. "It is to just such as these that the kingdom of God belongs. I assure you that whoever does not accept the reign of God like a child shall not take part in it" (Mark 10:14–15).

10

Jesus Christ Frees . . . and Divides

Another Kind of Peace

Do you suppose I came to establish peace on earth? No indeed, I have come to bring division [Luke 12:51, NEB].

The coming of Jesus the Messiah is a sign of great decisions. The introduction to the Gospel of John makes this clear from the very beginning: this event—his coming—is something extraordinary, because here indeed is the revelation of "the Father's only son, full of grace and truth" (John 1:14, NEB).

In Jesus the Father makes an incomparable and unrepeatable decision for his world and for his people. Through this decision old forms are affected in their innermost core, and the disorderly "order" of this world is totally overturned and made unstable. The Messiah brings a new understanding, and a new (because changed) reality.

God's decision for a changed world sets humankind before a similar decision.

God's decision about Jesus' coming forces humankind and the world into movement, because the decision is a powerful continuation of the liberation movement that he began with his people when he led them out of slavery in Egypt. And just as it was impossible for the pharaoh and the Israelites to withdraw from this movement inaugurated by God, so it was impossible for persons to withdraw themselves from Jesus of Nazareth.

Time and again Israel was confronted by God and faced the decision whether they wished to go further with him. Every time the choice had to be made anew: either further *with* God in faith to his promised land, or back to the reassurance of the fleshpots of Egypt. And later, when God had led them into the promised land, it was to be the same again. Then the choice was to be between Yahweh, the Living One, the Only One, and the idols; between trust in Yahweh and the temptation to follow Baal.

And each time this decision held the deepest repercussions for the people. And each time it brought dissension and division. So it was when Moses came down from the mountain and had to see how his people, while he was on the mountain struggling with God on their behalf, had begun to exchange, under the leadership of his brother Aaron, worship of God for worship of the golden calf. And then, once again, the challenge had to come: Moses "took his place at the gate of the camp and said, 'Who is on the Lord's side? Come here to me' " (Exod. 32:26, NEB).

So it was also when Elijah threw down the challenge to the prophets of Baal and thus also (how could it be otherwise?) to those who wished to be the people of God. How deep this decision cuts each time: "How long will you sit on the fence? If the Lord is God, follow him: but if Baal, then follow him" (1 Kings 18:21, NEB).

This is the same God who in the same movement of freedom throughout history calls persons, in his decision to give his Son, in his choice for humankind, to make their own decision and choice.

When Jesus comes, he brings a painful and controversial tension. Inevitably he causes confrontation with tradition, with powers, with persons. He comes into collision with sinful attitudes, wrong structures, and vested interests. When his parents brought him to the temple and sacrificed two turtledoves, Simeon prophesied: "Many in Israel will fall and rise again because of him" (Luke 2:34, NEB).

Confrontation with this Jesus makes it impossible for "the ordinary life" to run its normal course. His radicality with respect to the law, the Torah, the attitude of the Pharisees and the scribes,

bring him into conflict with tradition. His majestic association
with the poor and the oppressed, with harlots and tax collectors,
causes division among the people. His followers worship him as
Lord and thus come into collision with the Roman state and the
idolatrous emperor. He demands of his followers faithful obedience and total trust; he demands of them the capacity to take up
their cross, to regard everything else of lesser importance, and to
follow him. Father and mother, brother and sister, husband or
wife, are no longer all-important to his followers. Even the pres-
ervation of life is given a different, radical perspective by him:

> If anyone wishes to be a follower of mine, he must leave self
> behind: day after day he must take up his cross, and come
> with me. Whoever cares for his own safety is lost; but if a
> man will let himself be lost for my sake, that man is safe
> [Luke 9:23–24, NEB].

His hold on our lives is so total that all other human relationships have to be seen in another light. The word of the Torah,
"There is no other god besides me . . . ," becomes yet more radi-
calized in Jesus. And it is this fact that Jesus Christ is king, that *he*
has the last word over my life, that he rules over my total being—
that makes it so difficult for us, and brings division and fire in its
wake.

Therefore the division caused among us South Africans by "the
enlightened" and "the closed-minded," and the dissension
brought about in the churches by the Koot Vorsters and the Beyers
Naudés[1] (think, for example, of the battle over sports policies)—
all this is really nothing. The *real* issue has still to come!

In the squabbling about sports policies Dr. Vorster is of course
correct when he says that sports must not become an idol. This is a
very great danger in South Africa. But what is his alternative?
The idol of ethnic identity? The purity of the *volk?* How many
bloody sacrifices have already been laid on its altar in our history?
God is not yet even in this picture and the issues are not yet really
important. No, the real division has still to come!

When Christians in this country really take Jesus Christ and the
demands of the gospel seriously, then his fire and his sword will
become apparent. Then it will be seen how dissension will really

tear South Africa in two. But then at least it will be for *something,* for in the Bible the fire of which Jesus speaks is always a sign of purification. The fire separates the pure from the impure, and tests for what is lasting. Jesus says: "I have come to set fire to the earth, and how I wish it were already kindled!" (Luke 12:49, NEB).

He knows that he will have to go through this fire himself. He knows that he will not escape the testing and the purification, and "What constraint I am under until the ordeal is over!" (vs. 50). And the decision of those who go with him through the fire will bring division. Verse 51 can perhaps best be translated: "No peace, nothing but division." This shows how radical is this choice, how deeply it cuts, how final it is.

But how can Jesus say these things? What about the angels' message on the night of his birth? What of the song about peace on earth? What of the promise that his kingdom will be one of peace? Is there a contradiction here?

Justice and Peace

No, Jesus is not denying the angels' song. His critical words here apply to another kind of peace, the peace that is proclaimed and sung about when in reality there is no peace and there can be no peace. Just like Jeremiah in his time, so Jesus has no patience with the slippery merchants of piety who barter away genuine peace at the clerical market and try to palm off artificial products on the assembly of the Lord. Jesus desires a peace that is authentic. Not the sort of peace in which differences are patched over, sins are concealed, and irreconcilables are reconciled.

Jesus speaks of peace as the Old Testament understands it: God's longing that *shalom* should prevail on the earth. Shalom is the wish that things may go well with others. It is concern for the welfare of one's fellow beings. It is a sign of solidarity, of commitment to one another, of standing in for each other. In this peace, responsibility for each other—before God and before humankind—is embodied. In the Old Testament peace is always associated with right and justice. Peace is there as a *socio-political* reality.

It is in this kind of peace that swords will be turned into plowshares and spears into pruning knives. It is of this kind of peace that Jesus speaks. For this reason he opposes a superficial understanding of this word to which God himself has given content and meaning through his love and his liberation.

Peace, yes, but it must be genuine. Peace is not the power to pose a greater threat to the other with my better and more sophisticated weapons. Peace is not possible while thousands suffer hunger and the uprooting of communities and the destruction of families are glibly argued away with euphemisms such as "influx control."[2] There is no peace while millions are oppressed, and while right and justice openly stumble in public. There is no peace as long as conditions that give rise to hatred and bitterness, to repression and rebellion, are regarded as God-given. There is no peace while justified protest is smashed into the ground in the most brutal way. Let us not mislead ourselves: there is no peace.

The peace of God is different from the peace of the world. It is not only the absence of war, but the *active presence of justice.* And as long as injustice rules, no church and no Christian may not be at peace with themselves and the world. If Christians in South Africa are not purified in the fire of God's love, then we shall be consumed in the fire of his wrath.

The peace of God is a summons to battle with sinful structures, with those who resort to injustice, with the prejudice and sin in my own heart—with everything that obstructs his true peace. We have to make peace with him and with each other, and quickly too. To paraphrase for our situation the famous saying of Martin Luther King, Jr.: I am convinced that we shall still have remorse in our time, not only over the poisonous words and the detestable actions of evil persons who take no account of God and give his word no place in their lives, but we shall also have remorse over the horrifying silence and the indifference of the good persons who did not know "what served their peace."

If we are honest, we have to admit that the words which Jesus said in tears over Jerusalem also apply to South Africa:

If only you had known the path to peace this day; but you have completely lost it from view! Days will come upon you when your enemies encircle you with a rampart, hem you in, and press you hard from every side. They will wipe you out,

you and your children within your walls, and leave not a
stone on a stone within you, because you failed to recognize
the time of your visitation [Luke 19:42–44].

If only South Africa would listen so that we could know what
serves our peace. If a Christian people would only stop shouting
its own prophets down, ignoring them, shutting them up in
prisons where they are treated as if their lives were not worth a
cent. If Christian leaders would only stop glossing over evil,
thereby strengthening evildoers in their evil. If only we would stop
twisting, mutilating, and manipulating God's word to make it fit
the framework of the prevailing ideology. If only we could find
the courage to speak the truth to each other and not to mislead
each other for the sake of money or status, or out of fear.

It is painful, but we shall have to learn to accept that our obedience to Christ will also bring divisions within the church. We
shall not always have everyone go along with us. And it would be
wrong to sacrifice genuine peace for the sake of external con-
formity. We cannot indefinitely postpone doing what is right simply because not everyone is willing to go along with us.

Obedience and dedication to the Lord's work will bring division
and a lack of peace. And of course they will then take sides against
each other. But then it will no longer be on the grounds of race or
color or ideology, but on the basis of our willingness or unwillingness to follow the Messiah on his way through history. We seek not
the peace of the world, but *his* peace, the peace of him who has
made us one in him, and who has broken down the divisive wall of
hostility.

11

The King is Here!

Christmas

The angel said to them: "You have nothing to fear! I come to proclaim good news to you—tidings of great joy to be shared by the whole people. This day in David's city a savior has been born to you, the Messiah and Lord [Luke 2:10-11].

When I was preparing this sermon I found my thoughts going back to a song by the Dutch composer Jelle de Vries. In translation it goes something like this:

Merry Christmas, merry Christmas.
Don't worry too much about it;
Illusions and dreams must make way for tommorow;
Life must go on without it.

A lovely melody—but terrible words. Terrible, but nonetheless true. In the first place not because Christmas has become so commercialized, or because the emphasis in our Christmas celebration is so wrong—even if this is true—but especially because something is missing in the persons who turn their thoughts to Bethlehem with such noble intentions.

We approach the stable in an impressionable frame of mind and a tremendous romanticism grips us when we look at the infant in the crib. "Gentle Jesus, meek and mild. . . ." This may be nice, but it certainly is not the whole truth. And is this perhaps why Christmas is so easily tolerated and accepted by the world? Because nothing is affected or challenged anymore by this tremendous event? And if this is so, should we seek the fault in the world's poor understanding of Christmas, or rather in the fact that no one can see anymore why Christians should make such a fuss about it?

The Christmas event concerns a great deal more than just the birth of a sweet little child. It concerns the matter stated in our text: "a savior has been born to you, the Messiah and Lord."

Tidings of great joy, says the angel. Do not fear; *this* day there is born the Messiah, the Lord, the king. Today the promise of God has been fulfilled. Today he shows that he abides by his word.

The king is here; the liberator has come—because the word that we translate "savior" means "emancipator," "liberator," "redeemer."

What does it all mean? It means that God has—once again—made his choice for humankind. It means that he has refused to resign himself to evil, to sin, to our weaknesses.

In the beginning God spoke a word, a living and creative word . . . and in this word he called humankind to stand alongside him, to participate in his creation. And then the worst thing happened: humankind did not wish to hear, it turned its back on God, went its own way. It refused to hear God's word, and followed its own path.

With Christmas God speaks another word, a living word—*the* Word. In the birth of his Son it echoes through the heavens and over the earth: God's life-giving word for the lives of human beings.

God's word contains his *yes* and his *no*, and it is impossible to hear the *yes* without the *no*, and the *no* without the *yes*.

This word is God's *no* to sin, to the forces of darkness; it is his *no* to anger over humankind's infidelity. It is God's no to the twisting of our human intentions; to death, poverty, destruction; to exploitation, humiliation, and self-rejections.

But in Jesus the Word of God is also *yes*. God says *yes* to our creation, to health and happiness, to our growth and our human potentialities. In brief: *yes* to the burgeoning of the energies of our human existence.

In Jesus God addresses this word to us. And in Jesus he offers us a new life—a life that is not rent assunder by the contradictions of our human existence, a life that is *whole* in Jesus Christ, a life so poised between God's *yes* and *no* that in every *yes* the *no* is understood, and in every *no* the *yes*.

At Christmas God provided scope for humankind, scope for this new life, scope for a new creation. God says *yes,* and his *yes* takes on a regal form. Luke cannot stop multiplying the tremendous words to his readers: the liberator, the Christ, the Lord is here! Luke is saying, in effect: "It is true! The hope of the future is here! The promise of God is here! God is here! Emmanuel, God with us!"

The implications are deep and far-reaching. In the coming of the Messiah God is saying: "I am here, as I have always been, the eternal one, the faithful one, the liberator, the king." Christmas ruthlessly exposes the reality in which we live and to which we are prone to become accustomed, because it reminds us that God is greater than earthly reality. The established order must realize that the *real* king has now been born. Indeed, conflict is openly called for against the established order. Conflict with Herod, who saw his own position of power so threatened that he carried out the dreadful infanticide. And conflict with the emperor who was worshiped as "lord" and saluted with the title "savior of the people." Then comes the announcement: the *real* savior is here, the *real* king is here. The other king and the idolatrous emperor hear it; but so do the shepherds, and simple, God-fearing persons such as Simeon and Anna.

Now it becomes clear why the prophets could speak so freely and enthusiastically about the coming Christmas night. The undertones of the Book of Isaiah are like the distant rumbling of bad weather. It laments Israel's being unfaithful to God and deceiving him; it castigates the disparagement of others and Israel's deviation from the correct path. And then, suddenly, there is a song of the future, of a kingdom of peace and right and justice! Then once again Israel is in trouble, in exile, without hope, without a future; and again comes the word of God: "See, I will do something new!" (Isa. 43:19).

Isaiah 8 ends with a dismal picture: "They will pass through the land greatly distressed and hungry, and when they are hungry they will be enraged and will curse their king and their God" (8:21–22). And then suddenly: "The people that walked in darkness has seen a great light; they that dwell in the land of the shadow of death, upon them has a great light shone" (Isa. 9:1).

These sudden changes were possible because the prophets knew about and believed in God's supremacy, his kingship. The song of the prophets, of the reign of the Prince of Peace, becomes also the song of the angels: Peace on earth for the people of God's good will, because Christ, the Lord, is here. God is with his people. The Word has become flesh; the king is here.

This is the message of Christmas.

How is it possible that we could allow Christmas to become so watered down, so flaccid? Giving presents, being jolly, perhaps a trip to church—and then a huge dinner.

As if nothing had really happened!

Is Christmas really just a sentimental dream? An illusion that we should abandon as soon as possible because tomorrow normal life goes on again? Is there really no Christmas message to be spoken in Northern Ireland, where Christians are murdering each other and where again this year Christmas sermons will justify the violence? Is there no Christmas message to be spoken in Langa and Nyanga, over Guguletu and the squatter camps, over the many persons held in detention without trial and the thousands who are forced to keep Christmas hundreds of miles away from their wives and children? In this case there can be no question of Christmas being *celebrated*. Why? Because the law of the land makes it impossible.

Jesus the Messiah unmasks these conditions as inhuman and thus un-Christian; the power of those who cause them he calls false and idolatrous. It is the task of the church to make this word known without cessation: the Savior is here!

The Savior is here, and he frees us from our sins, from our fear, from hatred and bitterness, from self-conceit, from our self-disgust. He directs our eyes to his kingdom of righteousness and insists that we always live according to the laws of this kingdom.

In his life Christ was the liberator who never gave up the struggle against sin. He never resigned himself to it, and everyone knew it. The lepers, the sick, the lame, the prostitutes, the tax collectors, the poor, the oppressed, the despised. But also Herod, and the high priests. And when he breaks the bonds of death on Easter morning, then the last enemy himself knows it: the king is there! And then the resurrection: the sign of his victory and his lordship.

Those who confess the lordship of Jesus the Messiah do not acquiesce in the reality of this world. They know of the victory, and for them Christmas becomes the confession of their joy over the coming of the Messiah. It becomes the avowal of their own dedication.

We have a Christmas word, a glorious, liberating word. And we proclaim it today, tomorrow, and in the future: today is born the Savior who is Christ the Lord! And in this spirit we reach out our hands to each other and we wish each other "a blessed Christmas!"

12

The Finger of God

On the Information Scandal [1]

Then the magicians said to Pharaoh, "This is the finger of God." Yet Pharaoh remained obstinate [Exodus 8:15].

The heavens were opened and, as I looked on, a white horse appeared; its rider was called "The Faithful and True." Justice is his standard in passing judgment and in waging war [Revelation 19:11].

According to the church father Irenaeus, the Book of Revelation was written at the end of the reign of Domitian, the Roman emperor who turned the tradition of emperor-worship into a law. Under him the worship of the emperor became a legal requirement rather than merely a custom. It is thus understandable that tension in the Christian congregations increased at that time. The struggle between the Kyrios, Jesus the Messiah, and the temporal ruler, the emperor, became more pointed than before.

It also is understandable that proclaiming the word of God and professing Jesus as Lord frequently led to adversity. Can this be the reason—this continuing and sharpening clash between the Messiah and the emperor—why John, the minister of the congregation in Asia Minor, found himself in exile on the desolate island of Patmos, charged (was he ever formally charged?) and sentenced for proclaiming this "subversive" message: Jesus Christ is the Lord? (Incidentally, is it not noteworthy how totalitarian regimes since that time have shown a predilection for islands?[2])

However that may be, John is in banishment on the island of Patmos, apparently serving his sentence by command of the emperor. For him the conflict between Kyrios and Caesar has led to this point. But John knew and the congregation knew: precisely on this point the faith of the Christian congregation would have to prove itself. They would have to rise above their slave mentality and exchange their fear of the authorities for fear of the Lord. The conflicting loyalties were clearly spelled out: God or idol; Lord or emperor; Domitian the son of the gods, or the Son of God. Which name would be avowed?

John is now on the island. Offender, subversive, agitator, outcast.

But—and this is really tremendous—he is not there alone! God himself is keeping him company. And it is about these endless, wonderful colloquies with his God that John tells us in his writings. But there is even more. God not only talks with him. He lets John *see* as well. And not only that: he is allowed to see *what God sees.*

John sees what God sees.

As we open our chapter, John is describing what he sees: "And I saw the heavens opened. . . ." This time it is not, as in Revelation chapter 4, a door that is opened, but heaven itself. God does not merely give John a glimpse. He sweeps aside the whole curtain. Nothing is withheld from John's view. He is allowed to experience this moment in its fullness.

What does he see, this banned person? He sees the rider on the white horse, he sees the triumphal entry of the Messiah. This time the Messiah is not imaged in the form of a lamb, mute before its shearers and led without resistance to the slaughter. This time it is not the humiliated servant of God who is delivered over to the scorn and the violent high-handedness of tyrants. No, this time John sees the hero on a white horse. The king. The prince before whose majestic visage the glory of the idolatrous emperor will pale to the tawdry glitter that it really is. This time he does not

enter on a head-hanging, hollow-backed little ass. No, this time
he is mounted on a charger.

The Lord of Lords

And his name—this is something that John cannot speak
enough about in this chapter—his name is Faithful and True.

What kind of name is this? What other than *the* name! The
name that he received after his victory over death and the forces
of hell, the name above all other names. It is a name that recalls
the name: the echoes of the first announcement of the divine
name sound clearly here—*I am what I am.*

The firmness and the truth of this name had been discovered by
Israel centuries earlier. He is what he is, he will be what he will be,
in his association with his people, in the struggle with the pharaoh, in the emancipation from slavery, in the long, long trek
through the desert. In the words of the prophets, in Jesus of
Nazareth—in all this he showed that he had the power to do as he
promised, to keep his covenant. So he is called Faithful and True,
and now too he will do as he has promised, as he did before.

Presently John will say that only the rider himself knows his
name (19:12). But then John whispers the name in our ears:
"Word of God" (vs. 13). Eventually John will be able to contain
himself no longer and will jubilate: the name is "King of kings and
Lord of lords" (vs. 16). *That* is what he is! And the kings of the
earth? *He* is the king! The lords of the world, indeed!—those who
call themselves *baas* ("massa").[3] *He* is the Lord! Who still bows
down before Domitian? Who is still afraid of the pharaoh?

The pharaoh, like the emperor, was a son of the gods. Like the
emperor, he too was worshiped. He was like a god, with power
and status, this man who for so long decided the fate of nations,
including that of the people of God. By the time we come to Exodus 8, he had absolute rule over Israel and he denied God's people the destiny that Yahweh had in mind for them. He had decided
that God's plan for them would be foiled, because, after all, who
was this God? "Who is the Lord," the pharaoh asked scornfully,
"who is this Lord to whose voice I must listen?" (Exod. 5:2).

God wished his people to be freed, to become *his* once again.
The pharaoh refused. And he refused not only because he thought

he had the power to do so but also because he knew that God's liberating action for his people would mean the end of his own rule. On the grounds of his power and his continued rule he made his decision; he refused. Now, however, he had to take account of the power and the rule of the living God.

Hence the plagues. Little by little the undercutting of the pharaoh's rule. Ten times came the challenge. The continual undermining of his power, the exposure of his impotence, and, eventually, the public display of his insignificance. When the living God lifts his finger, the nakedness of the powerful is revealed. After the pharaoh, the baals and the dragons would discover the same thing. Even though there were seven plagues still to come, even though the earth would still have to become a valley of death before the pharaoh would give up the struggle, already he, the anonymous antigod of Exodus, was hearing from the mouths of his magicians: it is the finger of God!

This admission (in spite of themselves!) was made at this stage only by the pharaoh's magicians—the ideologues of the Egyptian court, the strategists of his propaganda, the inventors of the secret weapons with which he expected to defeat Israel and the God of Israel. They were the brilliant party conjurers, specially trained always to be one jump ahead of the others. They were the ones who had to realize, with great frustration and remorse, that their magic tricks no longer worked. They could only add one problem to another. They could aggravate the problem, but they could not solve it.

It was at this point that they realized with astonishment: "This is the finger of God!"

For the pharaoh himself it was still obscure, but it was soon to become clear to him also: ". . . as yet you have not listened. The Lord now says: This is how you shall know that I am the Lord . . ." (Exod. 7:16-17).

Note well that this is the same pharaoh who shortly before had said: "I know not the Lord" (5:2).

John sees it. The Caesar under whom the Lord's congregation was so heavily yoked would, despite all his power and glory, eventually have to admit that Jesus the Messiah is the Lord and more, that he is the victor.

And this victor would come to judge his enemies. No escape is possible. He judges and he wages war in righteousness. John leaves no doubt about the intentions of this victor-prince.

"His eyes blazed like fire," our translation reads, somewhat incorrectly. Literally it should be: "His eyes were a flame of fire." Once again the unequivocal, pictorial language of the Bible. It reminds us of the consuming fire from which Isaiah shrank back (Isa. 33:14); the scorching flame of which Paul speaks and which will eventually test all human works (1 Cor. 3:13).

For John it means that nothing is concealed from the Lord. He uncovers—in the sense of unmasks—everything. His eyes are a flame of fire—they burn with holy wrath and the fury of God, the almighty (Rev. 19:15b). And ultimately there is the sword—the sign of judgment and justice—that comes from his mouth to strike the nations.

So clear, fierce, and unavoidable is the judgment of the Messiah, the Lord of lords, the king of kings.

If his cloak is spattered with blood, it is the blood of his enemies, of the destroyers of his progeny, of the tyrants who with immeasurable arrogance dare to challenge the Kyrios. It is the blood of the pharaoh and his armies. Once again the Lord is the one whose finger is pointed in righteousness and judgment at the powerful who live on injustice.

The pharaoh, the baals, the emperor, the powers of today— they all see it eventually, the finger of God.

When Richard Nixon defeated Senator McGovern in 1972 it was one of the biggest victories by any politician in the history of the United States. President Nixon later interpreted it as a sanction or justification of his policies, policies that resulted in neglect of the poor in the U.S.A. itself and the escalation of the unholy war in Vietnam.

And there was something that passed almost unnoticed at that time. Just after the election a small book about McGovern's defeat appeared, with the significant title *Goodbye Mr. Christian*. For me it was the first indication of what could happen: this small book substantiated the thesis that it was not possible to practice Christian politics in "Christian" America. Was this book a pointing of the finger? I think so. And later there was the terrible Christmas of 1972 when the U.S.A. bombarded Hanoi in a manner in which even Nazi Germany had not acted during the Second

World War. Then many others saw what the president did not wish to see: the finger of God.

Watergate was merely a "last judgment," unavoidable, inescapable.

What we have been reading in all the South African newspapers recently about the escapades of the department of information and its officials has all the ingredients of a large-scale scandal. But for the Christian it is more than this: it is the finger of God.

It must be said that blacks are not at all surprised at the revelations that men in high government positions use immoral methods to defend the policies of their government to the outside world. In a certain sense the department minister and his subordinates could not do otherwise. When a policy is immoral in its essence, when violence is inherent in a political system, what else can one expect but that it has to be defended by immoral means and an escalating cycle of violence?

And besides, laws that clash with the gospel of Jesus Christ, laws that degrade and deny the human dignity of entire stratums of a national population, that separate husbands and wives from each other, that trample underfoot the most elemental of human rights—did any of us really think that God would allow all this to go on without punishment? And just like the pharaoh's magicians, these officials now begin to understand that their magic tricks do not work. With all their busy little schemes and plans all they could do was heap up problems for themselves. They could solve nothing, merely add plague on top of plague.

But it will get worse. What is happening here is more than just a symptom of corruption in one government department. It is more than just an indication of the immorality of certain government authorities. It is much more than just the demoralizing exposure of the hollowness and the spiritual bankruptcy of a particular political policy. At a deeper level it is the finger of God pointed at injustice and unrighteousness.

And it will get far worse. As did the pharaoh, government officials will harden their hearts and they will refuse to listen until the Rider on the white horse appears. What we are seeing now is the beginning of God's judgment on those who have long trampled his righteousness underfoot.

Believers see: this is the finger of God! But they see yet more:

they see the Rider on the white horse, the Lord, the Kyrios, the victor. It is he who rises above the powerlessness of his people and strikes the enemy with the judgment of his mouth. The people of God does not have to abandon its faith; it does not have to renounce the Messiah. Believers can be sure—despite the show of power and the sternness of the emperors of this world—that he is the Lord of lords, the King of kings.

And Jesus Christ is yesterday and today the same, and even unto eternity.

> After this I heard what sounded like the roar of a vast throng in heaven; and they were shouting: "Alleluia! Victory and glory and power belong to our God, for true and just are his judgments. He has . . . avenged the blood of his servants." Then once more they shouted: "Alleluia!" [Rev. 19:1–3, NEB].

Notes

Introduction

1. In this I agree with Colin Morris, *The Word and the Words,* London, 1975, Introduction.

2. See ibid, pp. 10–11.

3. The expression is from J. van Rooyen, *Durf ons Swyg,* Johannesburg, 1972, p. 35.

4. *The Word,* p. 17.

5. See the Terrorism Act, No. 83, of 1967, as amended by the Abolition of Juries Act, No. 34, of 1969, in *Statutes of the Republic of South Africa. Criminal Law and Procedure.* See also Geoff Budlender, "The Meaning of Terrorism," in *The Cape Times,* November 23, 1974.

6. See the interviews with young persons in *The Voice,* October/November 1976, p. 16.

7. H. M. Kuitert, "De Taal van de Prediking," in *Anders Gezego,* Kampen, 1970, p. 129.

8. This is the title of an arresting book by Prof. Manganyi, Johannesburg, 1972.

9. See C. Klapwijk, *Sociaal Masochisme en Christendom,* Kampen, 1975, a study that gives an excellent introduction to the thought of T. H. Reik.

10. The Afrikaans word *baas* is generally translated "boss," but its full political and emotional impact is better conveyed by the old American slave term "massa."

11. See the *Message to the People of South Africa,* Johannesburg: South African Council of Churches, 1968.

12. E. L. Smelik, *De Ethiek in de Verkondiging,* Nijkerk, 1967, p. 13.

13. See Allan Boesak, *Farewell to Innocence,* Johannesburg: Ravan Press, Maryknoll: Orbis Books, 1977, Chapter 1.

14. See Paul Lehmann, *Ethics in a Christian Context,* New York, 1963, p. 85.

15. Cited in ibid., p. 82.

16. A. A. van Ruler, "Structuurverandering in de verhouding Kerk en overheid," in *Theologisch Werk,* Nijkerk, 1972, Vol. 4, p. 131.

17. Ibid.

18. See André Biéler, *La pensée économique et sociale de Calvin,* Geneva, 1961. R. A. Meyer made some of this material available in *Pro Veritate,* May 1974.

19. Biéler, *La pensée,* p. 80.

20. Ibid.

21. In his famous speech "Sleeping through a Revolution."

22. Morris, *The Word,* p. 30.

Chapter 1

1. On October 19, 1977, the South African government announced its decision to ban eighteen black organizations, including the Christian Institute, and the black newspaper *The World.* In addition, an unusually large number of persons were banned, most of them black, all of them active in antiapartheid politics. A banned person is restricted to a specified geographical area, may not be quoted in the media, may not speak in public, and in fact is not allowed to speak with more than one person at a time. A banning order usually lasts five years, but can be renewed by the minister of justice.

Chapter 3

1. In 1838, during the era of colonization, Afrikaner (Boer) *trekkers* fought against the warriors of Dingane, the Zulu king. On December 16 of that year the Afrikaners made a vow, a "covenant" with God, that if he would give them victory, that day would be kept forever "as a Sabbath" by the Afrikaner nation. Their subsequent victory, therefore, was seen as an act of God, a sign of his favoring his chosen people. The river where the decisive battle was fought was afterward called Blood River, from the coloring that it took on during that battle. The event retains a powerful religious and nationalistic meaning for Afrikaners.

2. Riots broke out in Soweto, an all-black section of Johannesburg, in June 1976. They became a rallying point and symbol for all blacks in South Africa, and have been seen as a watershed in South African politics. In August of that year the children and young adults of Cape Town joined Soweto in a nationwide protest against apartheid.

Chapter 4

1. The theology of apartheid argues that both this text and the policy of apartheid affirm the God-intended diversity of races and peoples. It argues that the attempt to bring unity to the human race is akin to the endeavor of the builders of the tower of Babel, and thus rooted not in a God-given precept but in sinful human arrogance.

Chapter 5

1. See note 2, Chapter 3.

Chapter 9

1. The *Broederbond* ("circle of brothers") is a very powerful, secret organization of carefully selected Afrikaners. It controls South African society in an awesome way, reaching into politics, education, and the churches. Membership is secret and is sealed by a religious ceremony and solemn oath.

Chapter 10

1. Dr. Koot Vorster was for many years the most famous leader of the white Dutch Reformed Church in South Africa. A man known for his strong, uncompromising, right-wing attitudes, he was an unbending, articulate spokesman for, and symbol of, the extreme right in Afrikanerdom. Dr. Beyers Naudé is also an Afrikaner, but one who committed himself to the struggle for justice in South Africa. Once a powerful leader in the Dutch Reformed Church, he was defrocked when he became director of the Christian Institute, later closed by the government. Hated by most Afrikaners, he gained the respect of blacks. He was banned by the government on October 19, 1977.

2. "Influx control" is an expression used by the South African government in reference to its limiting the rights of blacks to reside in districts reserved to whites.

Chapter 12

1. In September 1978 it became public for the first time that the South African government's department of information had been using immoral means to "sell" the government's policy of apartheid to the

outside world. Large sums of money were used to bribe persons in high positions, phony organizations were set up, attempts were made to purchase newspapers (such as the *Washington Star*). The present sermon was preached after the first week of newspaper stories on the subject. Revelations would continue for months. More than a year later the minister responsible for the department had to resign, the state president had to resign, and there were other momentous changes, all of which caused great confusion in the country. The corruption that was uncovered was a heavy blow to Afrikaner pride and "sincerity."

2. In the South African context, the reference is to Robben Island and its infamous prison where the white government has imprisoned most of the black political leaders, among them Nelson Mandela, Walter Sisuiu, and the leader of SWAPO (South West African People's Organization) Herman Toivo ja Toivo.

3. See note 10, Introduction.

Scriptural Index

99

NEW TESTAMENT